E·A·S·Y
DECORATING

Heritage
House INC.®

THE SOUTHWESTERN COMPANY

Copyright© 1993 by Heritage House, Inc.
Publishing division of The Southwestern Company
P.O. Box 305141, Nashville, Tennessee 37230

Conceived, edited and published
under the direction of:

Chairman of the Board	Ralph Mosley
President and Publisher	Thomas Milam
Vice President of Marketing	Betty Ann Jones
Vice President of Operations	Ron Hartman
Executive Editor	Debbie Seigenthaler

Editor:	Mary Jane Blount
Managing Editor:	Robin Crouch
Creative Director:	Philip Sankey
Art Director:	Steve Newman
Project Leader:	Mary Cummings
Crafts Editor:	Kathleen English
Decorating Supervisors:	Miriam Myers, Fran Zinder
Photographer:	Bill LaFevor
Decorating Assistant:	Teresa Moll
Contributing Editors:	Kathryn Howard, Fran Morley
Associate Editors:	Linda Jones, Mary Wilson
Essayist:	Beverly Zelenka
Illustrator:	Barbara Ball
Typographers:	Sara Anglin, Jessie Anglin, Pam Newsome
Production Manager:	John Moulton
Manufacturing Assistant:	George McAllister

ISBN: 0-87197-386-3
Library of Congress Catalog Number: 93-11703

Manufactured in the United States of America.
First Printing, 1993

CONTENTS

INTRODUCTION   4

FAST AND FANCY WINDOWS   6
Minute Makeover—The Porch   28

CHILDREN'S PLACES   30
Minute Makeover—The Nursery   48

RECYCLED ACCENTS   50
Minute Makover—The Dining Room   56
Minute Makeover—The Bathroom   76

NO-FUSS FLOORS   78

EXTRA EASY WALLS   90
Minute Makeover—The Guest Room   108

ILLUSIONS OF SPACE   110
Minute Makeover—The Master Bedroom   124

NATURAL ACCENTS   126
Minute Makeover—The Kitchen   142

HOME PORTFOLIO   144

PROJECT INDEX   172

PHOTOGRAPH INDEX   174

INTRODUCTION

Nobody's home. For years, that's what we always said each time we drove by the abandoned house on the corner. Empty windows peered out between the dead tree limbs hiding the little house from full view.

Then, one spring, a thunderstorm swept away the branches, revealing a red brick facade smiling out shyly from behind years of neglect. Loose shutters, a sagging porch, weather-beaten paint—no wonder nobody was home.

One afternoon, we parked on the street and took our first tentative step onto the overgrown lawn. We trod over a moss-laden front walk and across the porch. Bob pulled a little peeling paint from the front entrance, and we discovered hardwood panels and brass hardware. Creeping through the unlocked door, I lifted an edge of moth-eaten carpet and found beautiful oak floors. Strong, solid walls and no water damage. From that moment, the house called to us.

Bob had heard that the out-of-town owner had long ago given up on the place and planned to tear it down to make way for a new duplex. Yet the house continued to hold our attention. We could see it had strong architectural features, a firm foundation, "good bones." And the backyard just beckoned for the children's swing set and Frosty's doghouse.

In answer to the house's call, we bought it. Our folks said we were crazy, that we'd spend a fortune fixing it up. But we knew that it needed only a little time, love, and elbow grease. Eventually, passersby would never say, "Nobody's home."

We would make it our home.

FAST AND FANCY WINDOWS

A unt Emily knows her jabots.

Many years ago, when my Aunt Emily tired of her heavy draperies, she hired an interior designer. After he told her the price of all-new window treatments, the designer found himself escorted quickly to the door.

So she came up with her own window solutions; some took only minutes and most didn't require sewing at all!

With bare windows of my own, I asked Aunt Emily to show me how she worked such wonders. She showed up at my backdoor, armed only with a hot glue gun, a stapler, and two bolts of fabric, ready to turn her dream designs into reality.

She draped fabric around the window frame and attached it to the top of the trim with a staple gun. She trimmed the fabric after it was hung, hemming with hot glue. On heavier fabrics, she just used pinking sheers and skipped the hem!

Her fabrics don't have to be expensive. She shops for remnants and flawed bolts at discount chains. Goodwill stores are her gold mines of window materials. Or she just buys muslin and paints tiny, evenly spaced stars or dots to get a name-brand look for a dollar a yard. My aunt also creates her own hardware with plumbing and lumber supplies!

And window treatments do not live by fabric alone. Aunt Emily covers her bedroom window with a painted piece of plywood cut to size. She hangs it like a picture from the top of the window, and she slips it under her bed each morning.

Use Aunt Emily's ideas and the quick no-sew techniques in this chapter to frame pretty pictures for yourself.

A charming window seat alcove transforms an ordinary bedroom into an inviting suite, beautifully framed with no-sew panels and valance swags. Turn to page 16 for directions to make this treatment for your home.

CRACKLE-FINISH DRAPE ROSETTES

The lovely effect of time on wooden pieces doesn't have to be generations in the making. It can be yours in a matter of hours. Crackle paint produces this antiqued texture on these rosette drape holdbacks, and gold paint highlights them with luster.

MATERIALS

Wooden rosette drape holdbacks
Black crackle medium
White acrylic paint
Paint brushes
Clear acrylic spray
Metallic gold paint

DIRECTIONS

Determine which sections of the holdbacks will be painted gold.

Following manufacturer's instructions, apply black crackle medium to portions of holdbacks that will not be painted gold.

Following manufacturer's instructions, paint white acrylic paint over black crackle medium. Allow to dry thoroughly.

Seal with clear acrylic spray.

Paint gold details, and allow to dry.

Seal with a second coat of clear acrylic spray.

Simply stunning cascades of fabric are hung from wooden dowels and rosettes, crackle-painted to match a striking candlestick grouping.
Easy reupholstered chairs pick up both the warm teal of the window fabric and the shimmering gold of the embellished napkin rings and floral container. Add these elegant items to your own dining room with directions found on pages 9–10 and 60–63.

Swagged Curtains

If you love the look of elegant curtains, but hate the cost associated with them, then we've got the perfect solution for you. A single length of fabric is draped across rosettes, finger-pleated into swags, and then stapled in place—the raw edges are hidden in pleats and puddles. Yes, that's right—no sewing machine is required either. To hang ours, we created Crackle-Finish Drape Rosettes using wooden drape holdbacks and a super lazy paint technique that produced an antique finish. Or, if you prefer, you can go to your local hardware store and locate a variety of rosette possibilities that are just perfect for this delightfully easy window treatment!

Materials

Rosettes
Mounting brackets
Fabric
Flat-headed thumbtacks
Staple gun and staples

Directions

Select rosette placement along window frame and mark placement positions lightly with a pencil.

Following manufacturer's directions, use mounting brackets to attach rosettes to frame.

Determine panel yardage by measuring the distance from floor to rosettes on each side of window, then add 16 inches to allow for puddling. Drape a tape measure across rosettes to determine desired drop in swags, and add to first measurement. (Note: Swag should cover about two-thirds of the top center windowpane.) This will be the total length of fabric you will need. Use the entire width of the fabric unless more or less fullness is desired.

Starting at left side of window, puddle fabric on floor and bring up to first rosette. Finger-pleat fabric, and drape over rosette.

Use thumbtack to hold fabric in place on mounting dowel of rosette. (Thumbtack allows for repositioning if needed.)

Bring fabric across to second rosette. Finger-pleat at a 45-degree angle to create the first swag. Make the top and bottom pleats as wide as the mounting dowel and inside pleats a little narrower.

Keep the top edge of fabric taut, and attach to rosette dowel with thumbtack.

Continue across windows to make all swags. Reposition if necessary.

One by one, remove thumbtacks as you staple fabric to rosettes on each side of window.

Bring the inside edge of the side fabric panel under the outer swag and staple to window frame under swag on each end.

Puddle fabric at floor.

Staple

BATHROOM CURTAINS

Boldly striped fabric adds drama to this bathroom window and shower curtain treatment. Using delicately carved gingerbread-style porch brackets available at the local hardware or lumber store gives added interest to the window. Silk ivy crowns both curtains and accents the tiebacks.

MATERIALS FOR WINDOW CURTAIN

2 wooden carved porch brackets
Wooden dowel to fit brackets
Wood saw
Paint to match window frame
Paintbrush
Fabric
Fabric glue
Decorative gold curtain rings
Tasseled curtain tieback
Artificial ivy

DIRECTIONS

Determine bracket placement, and measure length of dowel needed for rod. Cut dowel.

Paint brackets and dowel with 1 to 2 coats of paint. Let dry between coats.

Determine desired length and fullness of curtains, and cut fabric this size plus $1/2$ inch on all sides for hems.

(Note: Width of curtain in photo was $1^1/2$ times width of window.) Hem by turning to wrong side and gluing with fabric glue.

Attach curtain rings to top of curtain.

Mount brackets on window frame, slip curtain on rod, and hang curtain.

Drape curtain to one side, and catch with tasseled tieback. Arrange lengths of ivy along curtain top and tieback.

MATERIALS FOR SHOWER CURTAIN

Fabric
Fabric glue
1/4-inch plastic rings
Shower curtain rings
Artificial ivy

DIRECTIONS

Determine fabric yardage by measuring desired length and fullness of shower curtain. (This tub required 2 curtains to meet in center back.) Add 1/2 inch to sides and bottom for hem and 2 1/2 inches to top.

Turn under bottom hem and glue with fabric glue. Turn under side hems and glue in place. Turn top down 2 1/2 inches and glue in place.

Attach 1/4-inch rings to inside top of curtain, 2 inches from top edge.

Attach shower curtain rings to rod and loop small rings through shower curtain rings.

Arrange artificial ivy along top of curtains.

GATHERED SHEER CURTAINS

If you have some old sheers you'd like to reuse, this window treatment is a good idea, especially if privacy isn't an issue. By dropping them to half of the window height, sunshine and moonlight can stream in. And since not a stitch is required, this project goes together in a wink.

MATERIALS

Nails
Sheer curtains
Straight tree branch, width of window
Thread, string, or ribbon
Assorted artificial and natural materials

DIRECTIONS

Position 2 nails on each end of window frame to hold tree branch.

Fold sheers in half and drape over branch matching both ends of fabric at bottom. Gather bottom edges with thread, string, or ribbon.

Arrange artificial and natural materials along branch as desired.

POLISHED COTTON FLORAL AND STRIPED CURTAIN

A window treatment this elegant looks as though it could only come from a design shop. In fact, it's all done with staples and fabric glue and goes together quite easily. The polished cotton gives the curtain body, sheen, and impact, but the biggest surprise is how simple the detailing is to achieve. For our expensive-looking brass rosette, we used a discarded lampshade finial plate and a brass screw! Since the rosette does not support the fabric weight, any device for mounting the rosette will work to achieve this deceptively upscale look.

MATERIALS

Floral polished cotton fabric
Striped polished cotton fabric
Fabric glue
Staple gun and staples
Rosette and mounting device

DIRECTIONS

Determine yardage for swagged floral curtain by doubling the window width and doubling the window height. Turn short ends of fabric 1/2 inch to wrong side, and glue hems in place.

Gather center of fabric and finger-pleat loosely. Staple to top center of window frame.

Drape fabric loosely to each side, arranging to get desired swag and length on sides. Finger-pleat and staple to outer top edges of window frame.

Determine width and depth of pleated striped inset. Double width, and make panel by gluing a border of floral curtain fabric to striped fabric. Finger-pleat panel and staple inset to window frame under swags.

Attach gold rosette to top center of curtain or window frame.

A touch of ivy and raffia perfectly set off these "recycled" sheers, hung from a long, straight branch. Simple white sheers are folded in half, hung at mid-window, and knotted, creating openings above and below the treatment where light can filter through. Instructions appear on this page.

Easy Two-Fabric Jabot

This window treatment is so attractive and quick that you might want to change out the top curtain to suit the seasons, using rich tones for fall and winter then changing to pastels for spring and summer. See page 136 to use your own backyard flowers to top the treatment.

See page 136 to use your own backyard flowers to top the treatment.

MATERIALS

Tape measure
Fabric for undercurtain
Fabric for main curtain
Staple gun and staples
Nails
Straight pins

DIRECTIONS

Drape tape measure across window to determine desired drop in undercurtain swag and record measurement. Extend tape measure down side of window to the point where you want drape to end. Double that figure and add to swag measurement. Cut fabric this length plus 4 inches for poufed hems.

Repeat above to determine measurements for main curtain and add 16 inches for each corner knot. Cut fabric this length.

Position undercurtain on window frame, and staple top center to frame. Gather corners, adjusting swag, and staple to frame.

Hammer a nail into each corner of window frame, leaving $1/2$ inch extended to hold knot.

Position main curtain on window frame and style center of main curtain over undercurtain.

Determine position for knots on main curtain fabric at each corner, and tie simple overhand knots. Adjust knots as needed and catch knots on nails. Adjust fabric in swags and in knots as needed.

Turn all 4 curtain ends under, and catch on wrong side with pins to form poufs.

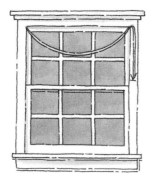

Both of these gorgeous no-sew window treatments are fashioned of inexpensive polished cotton. On the opposite page, a stunning windowscape is framed by a floral and stripe curtain, with instructions on page 12. At right, a double-hung window is set off by a two-fabric jabot topped with fresh dogwood, while the tablescape below features a floral bandbox and a silk lilac topiary. Instructions appear on pages 14, 15, and 69.

Window Seat Curtain

A rippled frame of fabric turns a window seat into a retreat. And despite the beautifully tailored effect, sewing skills are not required. Except for tacking gathers together on the valance swag ends, this curtain is hung with a staple gun!

Materials

1-by-4 pine boards
1-by-3 pine boards
Nails
Wood saw
Angle irons: 3 (2-inch), 4 (3-inch)
Mounting screws
Fabric
Hem tape
Needle and heavy-duty thread
Staple gun and staples

Directions

Measure width of window. Add 6 inches. Cut 1-by-4 this length for front of valance box. Cut 1-by-3 this length for top of valance box.

Nail front to top in L shape. Attach 2-inch angle irons to sides and center to keep square. Lay valance box aside.

Determine and mark position of 3-inch angle irons on wall, with 1 on each end and 2 evenly spaced between the ends. Attach irons to wall.

Determine fabric yardage: For side panels of curtain, measure from top of irons on wall to floor, and add 6 inches to each panel for puddles. For swag, measure valance box, and add 8 inches. Add 5 inches for center tab.

Cut fabric into 2 side panels, 1 top swag piece, and 1 tab piece.

Iron both long edges of tab piece 1 inch to wrong side, and secure with hem tape, following manufacturer's directions. Cut tab piece in thirds, and set aside. This yields fabric for 1 center tab and 2 tiebacks, if desired.

With 1 side panel piece of fabric, fold selvages 1 inch to wrong side and press. Gather 1 short end of panel desired width. Staple every few inches to front of valance box, referring to photograph. Repeat to hang other panel.

Center top swag piece on valance box with top edge of fabric extending 1 inch onto top of box. Begin stapling at top center point, and staple top of fabric along top edge of valance box.

Staple tab to backside of center of box with wrong side of tab facing forward. (When wrapped under and around swag, right side faces forward.)

Working on one end of swag fabric, finger-pleat ends up to bottom of box. Make sure bottom raw edge is concealed in pleats, and tack through pleats to secure. Pull fabric tightly to back of box, and staple. Repeat finger-pleat and stapling on other side of box.

Secure box to mounting angle irons on wall. Pull tab around center of fabric and staple in place on top of valance box.

Arrange swags, and puddle fabric on floor.

Herb-Accented Kitchen Sheers

Sheer curtains have stayed popular through all the decorating trends because they provide privacy while allowing light to pass through, and they do it without breaking the bank. If you like those qualities but want a way to jazz them up, look no farther than your refrigerator and garden!

Materials

Sheer fabric
Fabric glue
Curtain rod and rings
Vines and dried herbs
Twist-ties
Dried slices of oranges, lemons, and limes
Hot glue gun
Spring-type wooden clothespins

Directions

Measure and cut fabric for sheer curtains, adding 1/2 inch to all sides for hems.

Turn hems to inside, and glue with fabric glue.

Mount rod to top of window. Attach rings to top of curtains, and hang from rod.

Refer to directions on How to Prepare Vines, page 129. Secure vines along top of rod with twist-ties, tying loose, open knots at each end of rod, letting ends of vines cascade down.

Hot glue bunches of dried herbs and dried fruit to 2 clothespins for top corners of curtain. Clip herb swags to rod and fabric.

Hot glue dried fruit to several more clothespins, and use to ornament top of rod, to serve as curtain tiebacks, and to ornament baskets or other decorations in room.

DRIED FRUIT SLICES

Fruit has always inspired designers and decorators, and for good reason. Offering a wide array of colors, textures, and scents, fruit can be used whole or sliced, fresh or dried, and now, freeze-dried.

While freeze drying is not a home project, you can find a good selection of freeze-dried fruit slices through your florist. If you want to dry it yourself, however, the main thing you'll need is patience.

If you have a dehydrator, then you can obviously use that. But there are other ways. The trick is to use a dry, very warm environment so that the fruit dries rapidly. Otherwise, you can end up with rotten, moldy slices. You might want to experiment with small batches until you find the technique that works best for you.

If you have an attic that's stuffy in the summer, you can try it for suitability. Place a sheet of muslin on an old window screen, arrange a single layer of thinly sliced fruit on the muslin, and cover them with another sheet of muslin. Check them often.

You can also try using a warm oven, either one that was warmed and then turned off, or one that is warmed by a pilot light. Place the fruit on a rack over a cookie sheet to catch any drips.

And if Mother Nature is smiling on you, you can use a screen or rack in the hot, dry summer sun. Just watch out for hungry bugs!

Sheer Roman Blind

Unlined sheer black fabric gives this Roman blind an oriental feel. Roman blinds are more elegant than simple roll blinds, but offer the same simple tailored effect. A slight stiffness keeps the blinds crisp, so if you choose a soft fabric, you might want to iron it using starch or sizing before you begin.

Materials

1-by-2 board (for heading board)
Wood saw
Black sheer fabric
Hem tape
Ringed blind tape
Thread to match fabric
1/4-by-1 wood lath (for blind bottom)
Staple gun and staples
Screw eyes
Cord to match fabric
Cleat

Directions

Measure inside width of window. Cut 1-by-2 board this size. Measure window, add 3 inches to the width and 7 inches to the length, and cut fabric this size.

Turn sides of fabric 1/2 inch to wrong side, and press. Turn again 1 inch to wrong side, and secure with hem tape following manufacturer's directions.

Turn bottom edge of fabric 1/2 inch to wrong side, then 4 inches more, and press. Cut 2 pieces of ringed tape to fit on back of sides of blind, and place along inside fold line of side hems. Tuck into hem with bottom rings 1/2 inch from hem edge. Check to see that rings line up evenly across blind.

Open hem. Machine-stitch through all thicknesses on both sides of ringed tape.

Refold hem and machine-stitch 1/4 inch from inside edge. Make casing for bottom lath by stitching again 1 1/2 inches from first stitching line.

Cut 1/4-by-1 wood lath to fit just inside edges of blind in this casing, and insert. Slip stitch ends of hem to enclose lath and finish edges.

Lay 1-by-2 board on a flat surface and position top of blind along it, 3/4 inch from bottom edge and centered. Staple in place. This will be top of blind.

Insert 2 screw eyes on opposite side of board, each aligned with a row of tape. This will be bottom of heading board.

Cut 1 piece of cord 2 1/2 times the length of the blind. Cut 1 piece of cord 2 times the length of the blind.

Position blind right side down. Tie longest cord to bottom ring on your right and run through rings to top. Run through right screw eye, draw across header, and run through left screw eye.

Tie shorter cord to bottom ring on the left, and run through rings to top, running through the left screw eye.

Attach header board to window with screw eyes facing down. Gather cords and knot together along side of blind. Trim ends even.

Attach cleat to window frame. Raise blind to top, and secure on cleat. Leave raised for a few days to establish pleats.

A Roman blind echoes the decor of any room, whether formal or informal. Directions appear on this page.

Recovered Valances

If you want to give windows a fresh look without investing in a whole new treatment, here's a redo that works wonders. By recovering old valances, you can totally change the role they play in your decorating scheme. Deep tones can establish a balance in a light room with dark furniture, while lighter tones make the ceiling appear higher. Small patterns seem farther away, while bold patterns come forward to appear closer. If you have any doubts about how your idea will work, you can test the effect. Just drape sheets, bedspreads, or tablecloths that are similar to the fabric you're considering over the existing valances, then stand back to gauge the result.

How to Hang Mini-Blinds

Metal, plastic, or wood mini-blinds are a popular and decorative addition to any room, and they are easy to install.

The first step is to decide whether the blinds will hang inside the casement or outside, then carefully measure. If your windows are especially wide or long, you may need to consider custom-made blinds; however, most blinds are sold in ready-made sizes to fit the width of standard windows and can easily be adjusted to the proper length.

With a pencil, mark the position for the bracket screws. If the surface is plaster, start the screw by lightly tapping the end with a hammer; if the surface is wood, make a starter hole (slightly smaller than the diameter of the screw) with a nail or hand drill. If using a nail, be sure to wrap the head of the hammer with cloth so that the surface is not damaged when nail is pulled out. After the starter hole has been made, use a screwdriver to install the brackets, and snap the blinds into place. Let the blinds out all the way and lightly mark the underside of the slat that most nearly matches the correct length.

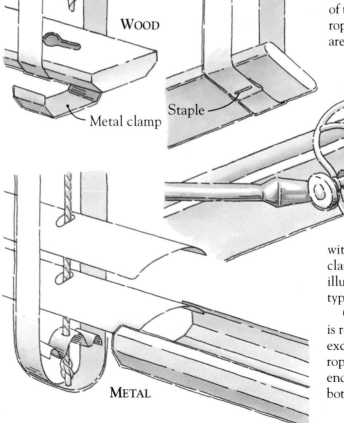

Wood

Metal clamp

Staple

Metal

Plastic

All blinds are shortened the same way, only the bottom bar is attached differently. On metal blinds, the bottom bar is hollow and simply slides over the last slat. With plastic blinds, use a utility knife or thin screwdriver to carefully pry out the buttons on the underside of the bottom bar. The ropes on wood blinds are usually held in place with staples or by a metal clamp. See the drawings illustrating each type of blind.

Once the bottom bar is removed, take off the excess slats, re-thread the ropes, trim and tie the ends, and re-connect the bottom bar.

MATERIALS

Sandpaper
Tack cloth
Fabric
Staple gun and staples

DIRECTIONS

Note: If the covering on your valances is not too dirty, textured, or dark, you can cover over them.

Take down valance, and remove old covering. Sand to remove old glue. Wipe with tack cloth.

Measure valances and determine fabric yardage, including enough to wrap under back side on bottom and around each end so that all visible surfaces are covered.

Lay fabric right side down on work surface, and center valance over it with open side facing you. Double-check fabric amount and positioning before you begin stapling.

Beginning at bottom of valance box, wrap and staple fabric to the inside.

Pulling the fabric smooth, wrap fabric over top of valance box and staple.

Wrap each end of the valance box as if wrapping a present, trimming excess fabric from corners so that ends do not become bulky. Pull fabric to ends of valance box and staple.

Reinstall valances.

STRIPED WINDOW VALANCE

Mini-blinds are practical and affordable ways to cover windows, but sometimes you want to add a little punch to your window decor. This simple painted valance does just that atop a kitchen window.

MATERIALS

1-by-6 pine boards
1-by-4 pine boards
Nails
Angle irons
Canvas fabric
Acrylic paint
Medium flat paintbrush
Spray fabric protector
Staple gun and staples

As easy as wrapping a present, these recovered valance boxes are recovered in thick woven plaid, providing a delightful contrast to a dry-brushed wall painting treatment. To redo your own valances, try the instructions on this and the opposite page.

DIRECTIONS

Measure width of window. Add 6 inches to window width to allow valance to extend 3 inches on each side. Cut one 1-by-6 pine board piece this length for front of valance box and one 1-by-4 pine board piece this length for top of box. Cut two 1-by-6 pine board pieces 3 inches long for box ends.

Nail top to front. Use angle irons at ends and middle to strengthen and keep valance square.

Nail both end pieces to valance. Set box aside.

Wash canvas to remove sizing, and press well.

Measure and cut a piece of canvas wide and long enough to cover valance box plus 2 inches on all sides.

Working on a flat surface, freehand-paint stripes on canvas with a light hand for uneven coverage. You may want to practice on a scrap piece of canvas first. Let dry. Spray with fabric protector.

Above, white mini-blinds are given a lift with easy-to-make valance boxes covered in plain canvas and striped with paint. Make your own using directions on pages 21, 22, and 23.

Lay canvas right side down and position valance box over it so that fabric will wrap correctly.

Beginning at bottom of box, wrap fabric to inside, and staple in place. Pulling fabric smooth, wrap canvas over top of box and staple. Wrap each end as if wrapping a present, trimming away excess fabric in folds. Wrap to inside and staple.

Check position on wall for angle irons to support valance at ends and attach angle irons to wall. If box is wider than 4 feet, attach mounting angle iron at center as well.

Position box on wall, and attach to angle irons.

Playroom Window Valance

This bright valance adds color above the sticky-finger line on this casement window. Its fabric not only coordinates with the toys and other decorations in the room, but also provided inspiration for the painted stepladder.

Materials

**1-by-3 pine boards
Wood saw
Nails
5 angle irons
Mounting screws
Fabric
Hem tape
Staple gun and staples**

Directions

Measure width of window. Add 2 inches. Cut 2 1-by-3 pieces this length for front and top of valance box.

Nail front to top in L shape. Attach 1 angle iron to each side and 1 in center to keep square. Set valance box aside.

Determine and mark position for 2 angle irons on wall, with 1 at each window corner. Attach irons to wall.

Determine fabric yardage: Measure valance box, and add desired length of side drops to this measurement. Add 4 inches for hems.

For 2 tabs, cut 1 piece of fabric to measure 6-by-56-inches. Press long edges $1/2$ inch to wrong side and secure with hem tape, following manufacturer's directions. Cut fabric strip into two 5-by-28-inch pieces.

Once the valance box is nailed together and mounted, these gorgeous curtains are made and hung in about $1^1/2$ hours! Full instructions appear on this page.

Press all sides of curtain fabric $1/4$ inch to wrong side, then $1^3/4$ inches to wrong side, trimming excess fabric from corners. Secure on all 4 sides with hem tape.

Center fabric on box with top edge of fabric extending 1 inch onto top of box. Begin stapling at top center point, and continue stapling top of fabric to box.

Staple tabs to backside of box front at ends with wrong side of tab facing forward. (When wrapped around swag, right side of tab will face forward.)

Secure box to mounting angle irons on wall.

Pull tabs around fabric on ends, arranging folds as desired. Staple tabs in place on top of box.

Puddled Curtain with Rosettes

Sometimes you want curtains that have impact without blocking light or overpowering the rest of the room. This draped ecru curtain, gathered in rosettes and puddled on the floor, adds a strong dose of elegance without becoming heavy. You'll need a partner to create this project.

Materials

Nails or wood screws
Fabric
Thin wire or string

Directions

Decide where rosettes will go on window frame, and insert nails or screws at those points, leaving head about $1/2$ inch extended from wall.

Determine fabric yardage by adding together the following: distance on both sides of windows from floor to nail, plus 6 inches for each puddle, plus the distance between rosettes, plus 12 inches for each rosette.

Measure distance from edge of puddle to nail at left corner of window, and grasp fabric at that point with left hand. Grasp fabric 12 inches from left hand with your right hand, and station your partner nearby to assist if necessary.

Finger-pleat 12-inch segment, and bring hands together in back to fold in half. Have your partner wrap wire or string around fabric.

Gently pull pleats into rosette, opening pleats and tucking edges under. Push rosette on nail.

Repeat across window to make and attach rosettes, draping pleated fabric between rosettes as loosely or tightly as desired.

Conceal all raw edges in folds, and arrange puddles on floor with raw edges turned under.

Tone-on-tone window and wall treatments combine with little romantic touches to create an enticing bedroom decor. Perfect complements are delicate pillows made from old linens and botanical prints with customized mats. You'll find directions for these lovely design elements on pages 24, 66, 67, 98, and 100.

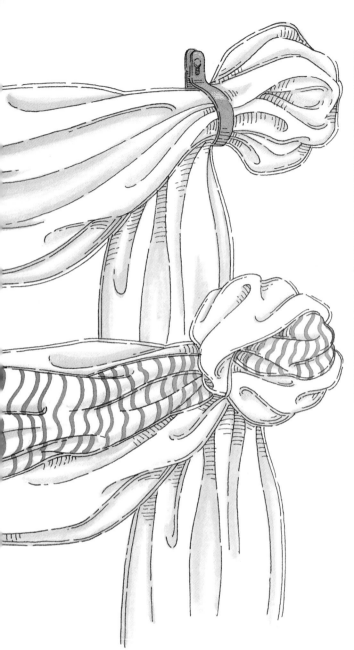

No-Sew Curtain

We wandered into the plumbing and fencing departments at the hardware store to find the inexpensive materials for this curtain rod. You'd never know it, though, looking at the gentle swag and delicate corner rosettes that descend into cloud-like poufs.

MATERIALS

Metal fence connecter rings
3/4-inch diameter PVC pipe
Twin sheet for main curtain
Twin sheet for coordinating center swag
Safety pins

DIRECTIONS

Screw metal rings into each end of window frame. Measure and cut PVC pipe to correct width, and insert through rings.

Determine desired drop in curtain swag and length on sides, add 24 inches for each rosette, and cut sheet for main curtain this length.

Fold in half lengthwise, and center on rod. Pull ends through metal rings, arranging center swag as desired.

Pull ends of fabric back through rings leaving enough fabric looped at each ring to make a rosette.

Arrange sheet for coordinating center fabric over swag, and pull through rings to form loops for rosettes with main fabric. Arrange rosettes, hiding raw edges of center fabric in knots. Secure with pins on wrong side.

Turn curtain ends under, and catch on wrong side with a safety pin to form poufs.

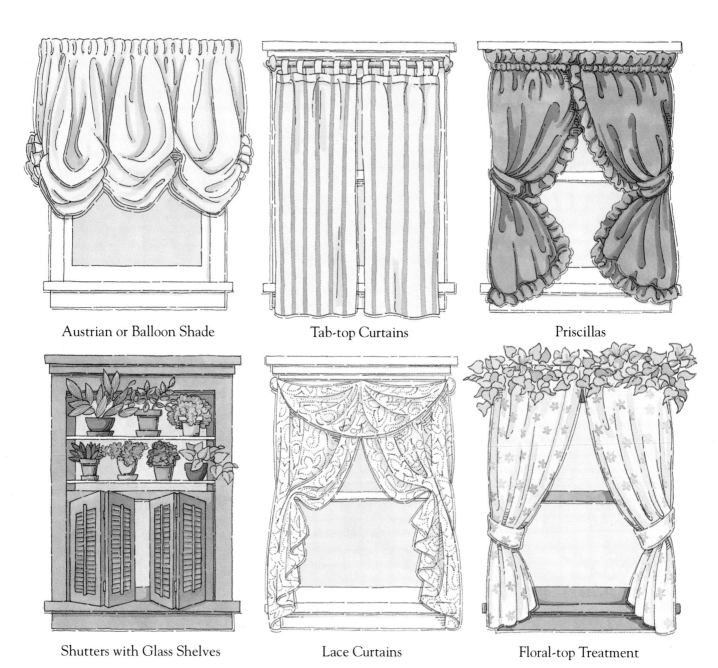

Austrian or Balloon Shade

Tab-top Curtains

Priscillas

Shutters with Glass Shelves

Lace Curtains

Floral-top Treatment

Window treatments are an integral part of a decorating scheme. Windows that are beautifully dressed enrich the style of a room. Some provide a subtle backdrop for other elements in the room, while others are the focal point. From breezy, Austrian shades, to draperies with floral top treatments, the choices are endless.

When you are deciding on the type of window treatment to use, consider the style of the window. Some window treatments may not be suitable. Some slide up and down, some slide sideways, and still others swing in or out. If you want to open and close the windows for air, select window treatments that will not get in the way. If you have casement windows, the window treatment must not interfere with protruding handles that operate the windows.

Remember, the fabrics and hardware you select affect the formality of the treatment. A lace curtain may look elegant, while a tab-top curtain with a wood pole has a casual, informal look. Don't over-look shutters as a window treatment. They can be a beautiful complement for your woodwork.

The Porch

This airy outdoor room beckons with a cozy conversation area, sumptuously surrounded by natural accents and filled with bright yet inexpensive pillows and cushions.

The promise of evening allures with a wide variety of light sources from surprising objects containing votive candles — a hole-punched watering can, a moss-filled terra cotta pot, and two painted and hole-punched coffee cans.

An easy-to-make wreath and stick bird cage brings the outdoors in and is complimented by simple pots and planters embellished with raffia and filled with painted sticks and twisted twigs. Notice how the texture of the stiffened potato sack restates this outdoorsy theme.

A large piece of cotton canvas, painted with easy striped and checkered borders, picks up the fabric colors and pulls the furniture together, bringing the whole design scheme into one.

The basics were already here to make this porch an outdoor paradise. All that was needed were the accent pieces—pillows, plants, light sources—to tie the room together and make it both beautiful and comfortable.

CHILDREN'S PLACES

His, mine, and ours. That's what I call our four kids, who range in age from two to sixteen. And trying to provide each of them with enough space over the years has become quite a challenge in our small home.

Among the best solutions for privacy I've found are screens, which can be used to divide shared bedrooms, giving each youngster a place to call his or her own. I have tried brightly painted lattice work, scrunched sheets glued to plywood, wallpaper-covered bi-fold doors, even Army surplus camouflage netting lashed to and hung from dowels as privacy screens.

To give the children's rooms a sense of individuality, we've borrowed themes from their linen sets. The circus sheets in our youngest children's room expanded into a family project. Our teenager painted animal faces on the baby's dresser drawers, using knobs as noses. A bright, wide-striped patio door curtain, found for five dollars in a consignment shop, yielded enough fabric for all four windows! Bob outlined a circus wall mural in black paint and let the children "color" it with washable acrylics. To complete the look, we tacked two popsicle-stick and jute trapezes to the ceiling and perched clown-suited monkeys on them.

After his, mine, and ours no longer "belong" to us, I believe they'll have learned alot from our working together to create their own personalized places to call home. They'll each have an appreciation for privacy, a sense of individuality, and a touch of creativity to pass along to their own families.

A whimsical stepladder and no-sew valances turn a former one-car garage into a kid-friendly playroom with bright colors and geometric shapes. Turn to pages 23 and 33 for simple instructions on creating these fun projects.

Giant Origami Figures

Use one of your child's origami books, or find one at the local library, and enlarge the designs to create eye-catching decorative accents. Try a flock of birds, or maybe a grouping of dinosaurs. Origami in bright, primary colors is perfect for children's areas, but simple black, gold, or white figures will compliment even the decor of a master bedroom suite or a living room.

MATERIALS

Origami book
Large pieces of butcher paper
Fishing line, if desired

DIRECTIONS

Follow instructions in book on a larger scale to make oversized origami figures. If desired, hang from ceiling with fishing line.

Papier-Mâché Bowls

The timeless craft of papier-mâché is a great way to introduce children to the joys of creation. A simple bowl can become a treasured dinosaur nest, a gift for Dad's dresser, or just a thing of beauty to add color and sentiment to playroom shelves.

MATERIALS

Balloon
Scissors
Newspaper
Liquid starch
Cardboard tube, paper cup, or cardboard scrap
String
Acrylic paints and paintbrush, if desired
Paper cutouts or stickers, if desired
Clear-drying craft glue, if desired
Tissue paper, if desired
Polyurethane sealer

DIRECTIONS

Blow up balloon to desired size for bowl, and tie end tightly.

Cut newspaper into 1-inch wide strips 2 to 4 inches long.

Pour liquid starch into a container. Dip newspaper strips in starch, and cover balloon, leaving about 2 inches around knot uncovered. Lay strips at different angles, and build up 3 or 4 layers.

Cut a piece of cardboard tube for base, or use part of a paper cup or a strip of cardboard taped into a tube. Cover tube inside and out with newspaper strips dipped in starch. Position base on ball opposite tied end, and cover with more layers of newspaper strips to attach tube to ball.

Hang balloon from string, and allow to dry for several hours.

Untie balloon, and remove from ball. Allow inside of ball to finish drying.

Mark top edge of bowl on ball, and cut along this line with scissors.

Decorate bowl by painting designs with acrylic paint, gluing on paper cutouts, using stickers, or crinkling and tearing tissue paper and gluing over surface for texture.

When decorations are finished and dry, seal all surfaces of bowl with 1 or 2 coats of polyurethane.

Painted Sticks

Crayon colors transform simple sticks into a whimsical decorating accent. Choose colors to match the room—or if you're making other items for the room, use a bit of the leftover paint for a perfect match.

MATERIALS

Handsaw
Bundle of sticks
Acrylic paints
Paintbrush
Container

DIRECTIONS

Use a handsaw to cut off ends and side branches from sticks.

Paint each stick a solid color, and let dry.

Paint stripes around sticks in bright colors, allowing each color to dry before beginning to paint a new color.

Arrange painted sticks in container.

Toy Storage Tubs

Keep those toys and collections together by organizing them in see-through plastic tubs. The large bright lettering will be a start on the road to reading for preschoolers, and this method of organization should help make pick-up time easier for everyone.

Materials

Large plastic see-through tubs with lids
Vinyl adhesive letters
Stickers, if desired

Directions

Label tubs with letters.
Embellish with additional stickers if desired.

Painted Stepladder

Reaching for books and toys is a joy when you have a happy stepladder always in reach. This unfinished stepladder is widely available, and it conveniently converts to a chair. The paint job plays on the colors and geometric shapes from the curtains of the room, adding a bold decorating note both in use and on display.

How to Improve a Child's Closet

If your child is old enough to put away his or her own clothes, the installation of an additional shelf and hanging rod in the child's closet will add much needed storage space and be a big help to Mom.

Measure up from the floor the child's height plus eight inches and mark along the back and both side walls of the closet. Measure the distance from wall to wall and the depth of the side walls. The hanging rod should have at least twelve inches clearance in front and back; measure, choose, and mark its position on both side walls.

At the lumber yard, have a 1-by-4 board cut into two pieces, each the planned depth of the shelf; have a 1-by-2 board cut to fit across the back wall. In addition, have shelving cut to fit and a wood or metal pole cut to fit the width of the closet. You will need two sockets to fit the diameter of the pole.

Following the lines made earlier, nail 1-by-4 boards into place on the side walls. If you cannot nail into wall studs, use expanding nails to hold boards firmly in place. Measure again, and install the sockets. Nail the 1-by-2 board to the back wall, being careful to line it up with the boards on the side walls.

Fit the wood or metal pole in place, and position the shelf over the wood supports. If the pole is more than three feet long, a center support will be necessary.

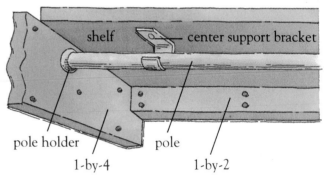

shelf — center support bracket

pole holder — pole

1-by-4 — 1-by-2

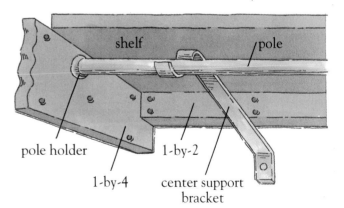

shelf — pole

pole holder — 1-by-2

1-by-4 — center support bracket

MATERIALS FOR PAINTED STEPLADDER

Wooden stepladder
Fine sandpaper
Tack cloth
Wood primer
Paintbrushes
Acrylic paint in desired colors
Masking tape
Polyurethane sealer

DIRECTIONS

Lightly sand all surfaces of stepladder, and wipe clean with tack cloth. Paint with primer, and let dry.

Paint base color, and let dry.

Mask off random squares over surface of stepladder. Paint inside masked area. Let dry. Add additional painted details as desired, allowing paint to dry between coats.

Seal with 2 or 3 coats of polyurethane, allowing sealer to dry between coats.

SPATTERED CHAIR AND STEP STOOL

This is an excellent way to take an odd chair and step stool and create coordinated furnishings. The chairback detailing is just enough to carry the room's theme without becoming too busy.

MATERIALS

Chair
Step stool
Liquid deglosser
Acrylic paint
Paintbrushes
Old toothbrush or small stiff brush
Metal knife
Tracing paper
Carbon or graphite paper
Polyurethane sealer

An unpainted stepladder/chair becomes a conversation piece by simply borrowing a pattern from the curtain fabric in this playroom. Labelled stacking toy bins are stickered in the same bright colors echoed by a bouquet of painted sticks. For more details, see pages 32, 33, and 35.

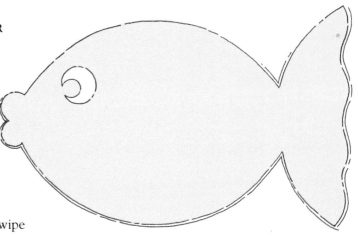

DIRECTIONS

Thoroughly clean and dry surface of chair and step stool. Apply deglosser to prepare the finish for painting.

Paint with a base color, and let dry.

Apply a second coat of paint if needed. Let dry.

For spattering, thin paint with water to a milk-like consistency.

Before spattering furniture, practice technique on a scrap of wood or cardboard.

Dip the toothbrush in paint. Sweep the metal knife toward you across the bristles to create spatter.

For larger spatters, knock the brush sharply against the knife.

Continue layering spatters over chair and step stool to get desired effect.

Let paint dry completely.

Choose a pattern from wallpaper, and trace onto tracing paper.

Position pattern on chairback and place graphite paper under it. Trace pattern to transfer to chair.

Repeat to create grouping of elements on chair, if desired.

Paint patterns in desired colors. Let dry.

Seal chair and step stool with 2 coats of polyurethane, allowing sealer to dry between coats.

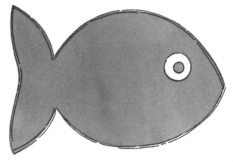

BOUNTY FROM THE SEA

Schools of fish on brightly colored wallpaper provide the inspiration for this basement turned child's room. Several clever tricks with wallpaper are combined to make the most of the materials.

First is the use of two wallpaper patterns and a border. In the bedroom, the wall is divided into three sections by the border used in two places. By placing a smaller pattern in upper areas, the ceiling seems higher. But the bold border brings the scale down to better fit a child's perspective. The larger pattern fills the lower portion of the walls and wraps onto the built-in storage bench to better unify the space.

In the bathroom, the larger fish dot pattern covers the entire wall, but the dropped border achieves the same effect of both raising the ceiling and scaling down the room to a child-sized space.

To add polish, the border is framed in both rooms by molding that is pickled to match the other molding in the room.

Finally, the sea creatures in the paper patterns are used to decorate other elements in the room.

FISHY LAMPSHADE

Here's a quick way to use leftover scraps of wallpaper and coordinate a lamp. This shade goes together in minutes, and it is a project that even inexperienced paperers can attempt with success.

MATERIALS

Tissue paper
Lampshade
Wallpaper scrap
Wallpaper paste
Brush or roller
Craft knife

When families outgrow their living spaces, basements can become beautiful children's rooms. This basement bedroom carries an underwater theme with gorgeous wallpaper, its colors echoed by spatter-painted furniture, a madeover lampshade, and a finger-painted switchplate. Use these ideas with patterns and instructions on pages 35, 36, and 39.

DIRECTIONS FOR FISHY LAMPSHADE

Wrap tissue paper around lampshade, and mark edges of shade to make pattern. Cut out.

Position pattern on back of wallpaper scrap. Transfer to wallpaper, adding 1/2 inch at top opening and along bottom edge and adding 1/4 inch on end for overlap.

Cut out wallpaper.

Use a brush or roller to apply wallpaper paste to back of paper.

Position paper on shade, smoothing into place. Wipe off any excess paste with a damp sponge.

Cut tabs of paper on top and bottom at 1/2-inch intervals from outside edge of paper to edge of shade.

Wrap tabs to shade back; press firmly in place. Let dry.

(If the shade has a raised lip at the top and bottom, trim the paper to end at the lip.)

STARFISH SWITCHPLATE

Let your child have a hand in the decorating process. This sea creature is finger-painted onto a spattered surface. Just be sure you supervise so that paint goes where it's supposed to and not into mouths or on clothes.

MATERIALS

Switchplate cover
Fine sandpaper
Acrylic paints
Medium flat paintbrush
Old toothbrush or small stiff brush
Metal knife
Polyurethane sealer

DIRECTIONS

Whether you are using a plastic or wooden switchplate cover, begin by lightly sanding the surface for better paint adhesion.

This teenager's room offers its own private study hall tied into the decorating scheme with a simple wallpaper border surrounding an inexpensive painted bookcase, table, and folding chair.

Paint with basecoat color, and let dry.

Spatter switchplate with paint following directions for chair and let dry.

Allow child to pick out a design and color, and have him or her finger-paint it on the center of switchplate. Let dry.

Finish with 2 coats of sealer, allowing sealer to dry between coats.

SPATTER-PAINTED MEDICINE CABINET

It's easy to coordinate a mirror into a decorating scheme like this one, even if you're working with a medicine cabinet. If the frame is wooden, simply mask off the mirror, and refer to the spatter-painting directions for the chair on page 35.

If the frame is metal, you'll need to lightly sand the surface, and paint it with a metal primer before continuing. Since the mirror will be subject to steam and humidity, it's best to use exterior metal paints to create the design.

In either case, a good sealer is the final step. Choose one that's compatible with the materials used for painting, and apply at least two coats.

LASSO TRASH CAN

Round up stray trash with this lasso trash can. Any large plastic tub or can will do as a base, making it as economical as it is clever.

MATERIALS

Heavy jute rope
Large plastic tub or can
Hot glue gun
Craft knife

DIRECTIONS

Begin coiling rope at bottom of outside of can, and secure to can with hot glue.

Conceal beginning end of rope under the next coil of rope, and work up to top continually securing with hot glue. Leave 12 inches of rope at top. Repeat on inside, making a smooth rim at top. Tie excess rope in a knot, and trim to finish.

Covered Wagon Bed Canopy

Encourage that pioneering spirit with a covered wagon canopy. Mount it above the headboard, or use it in place of a headboard, positioned high enough that little heads won't go bump in the night.

Materials

45-inch wide canvas
Hem tape
Thread to match canvas
2 flexible drapery rods with mounting brackets

Directions

Determine canvas yardage by measuring width of bed and adding 17 inches. Press short ends under $1/8$ inch, then $1/4$ inch. Secure with hem tape, following manufacturer's directions.

Turn long ends $1/4$ inch to wrong side and press. Turn ends under $1^1/4$ inches, and machine-stitch 1 inch from edge to form rod casings.

Determine where bottom of canopy will be, and mount 2 brackets there. Mount other pair of brackets 4 inches above first pair.

Insert rods in canopy casings. Bend and attach rear rod to top brackets and lower rod to bottom brackets. Using pliers, carefully turn bottom brackets to desired angle out from wall to create canopy effect.

High Plains Mural

Set the stage for sweet dreams of roundups with this desert mural. You can draw your inspiration from children's books, encyclopedias, movies, or even fabric patterns. Be sure to note the position of the bed and use it as a reference as you work. The simpler you keep your design, the more effective it will be.

What little cowboy or cowgirl wouldn't be thrilled with this room. The wall mural turns three-dimensional with the addition of a canvas-covered wagon canopy, and a pleasant accent piece was made in a matter of minutes by covering an inexpensive trash can with rope.

The resident of this room can be assured of pleasant dreams each night as he or she goes to sleep on this open frontier. Instructions are found on pages 39, 40, and 43.

MATERIALS FOR HIGH PLAINS MURAL

Latex wall paints: sky blue and sand beige
Paint roller and paintbrushes
Graphite paper, if needed
Acrylic paints for scenes
Clear latex polyurethane

DIRECTIONS

Paint top of wall sky blue, and let dry. Freehand paint horizon line with sand beige paint, and paint lower half of wall sand color. Let dry.

Choose designs and either sketch freehand or transfer with graphite paper to wall.

Paint designs, thinning paint if a washed effect is needed and using full-strength for solid areas. With overlapping colors, let base coat dry before applying overlapping coat. Seal with polyurethane.

BANDANA CURTAIN

Bandanas are good for many things—keeping the dust out of your lungs on the trail, protecting your neck from the sun, or covering your window!

MATERIALS

Stick
Bandana
Black embroidery floss or leather lacing
Tapestry needle
Long finishing nails

DIRECTIONS

Measure width of window. Choose a stick or tree branch that is 4 inches longer than window width.

Fold bandana diagonally, center on stick, and tie bandana ends around stick.

With embroidery floss or leather lacing, lash folded edge of bandana to stick.

Nail ends of stick to window with finishing nails.

A study corral features a rope-covered trash can, rag-painted desk, cowboy boot lamp, cactus garden, bandana curtain, leather-look pencil holder and cowboy picture frames, with instructions appearing on pages 39, 43, 44, 45, and 137.

LEATHER-LOOK PENCIL HOLDER

You can make this pencil holder in a few minutes the next time you sit down to polish your shoes. Just add masking tape and a can to the assembly line of shoes. Torn strips of tape, lightly coated with brown polish, give the appearance of leather to a pencil holder fit for a cowboy.

MATERIALS

Metal fruit or vegetable can
Pliers
Wide masking tape
Brown shoe polish
Cloth rag

DIRECTIONS

Bend back and smooth any raw cut edges on can with pliers. Clean and dry can thoroughly.

Tear masking tape into irregular pieces, and apply them randomly over entire can, inside and out.

Overlap pieces, and add as many layers as needed to get desired effect.

Apply a heavy coat of shoe polish to holder with rag. Wipe off excess and let dry.

RAG-PAINTED CHILD'S DESK

Brighten up study time with a bit of paint magic. The technique used here is ragging, with two similar tones of gold used to produce a parchment effect on the desk top and drawers. By changing the bright red knobs to another shade later, you can totally transform the look of the desk, making it work well in a more mature setting.

MATERIALS

Desk
Fine sandpaper
Tack cloth
Wood primer
Acrylic paints in desired colors
Ragging cloth or plastic wrap
Clear polyurethane sealer
Red acrylic paint

Directions for Rag-Painted Child's Desk

Pull out drawers from desk and remove knobs. Lightly sand all surfaces to be painted and wipe clean with tack cloth.

Paint with wood primer, and let dry.

Paint all solid areas on desk, and let dry.

Refer to directions on How to Rag with Paint, page 101, for only desk top and drawer fronts. Let dry.

Seal desk with 2 coats of polyurethane, letting dry between coats.

Paint drawer knobs red. Let dry. Seal with 2 coats of polyurethane, letting dry between coats.

Reassemble desk.

Cowboy Boot Table Lamp

Throw some western light on study time with this lamp made from a cowboy boot. If you don't have a spare boot yourself, you can pick one up at a yard sale or flea market. Either use an old lamp for the mechanism, as we've done, or buy a lamp kit and install it in the boot.

MATERIALS

**Small lamp or lamp mechanism
Cowboy boot
Drill
Lampshade
Muslin or burlap fabric
Craft glue**

DIRECTIONS

Refer to directions on How to Wire a Lamp, page 45, and detach top of cord from existing lamp or mechanism.

Unless boot already has a serviceable hole, drill a hole in the sole near heel for cord.

Run cord through hole and reattach to lamp or mechanism. Place lamp or lamp mechanism inside boot.

Recover lampshade by wrapping muslin or burlap around existing shade and securing fabric with craft glue. Fit shade on lamp.

Cowboy Frames

Your little pardner will love seeing his heroes' pictures posted in these leather-look frames. Since many of these steps are easy to do, you might want to sign up a young deputy for assistance.

MATERIALS

**Craft paper
Tempera paint in desired colors
Foam brush
3/16-inch thick foamboard
Right angle
Metal straightedge
Craft knife
Craft glue
Acetate
Masking tape
Thin cardboard
Easel back or picture hanger
Conchos, nailheads, and other western trims
Suede or leather lacing, if desired**

DIRECTIONS

Cut a piece of craft paper twice the size of desired frame. Tightly crumple, then smooth paper.

Spread paint over surface with foam brush. Rinse quickly and let dry. Add additional colors if desired. Let dry between coats.

Draw frame on foamboard, using a right angle to mark corners and to keep square. Repeat to mark openings.

With metal straightedge, cut out frame, keeping knife blade straight at all times.

Apply a thin coat of glue to 1 side of frame. Center paper over frame with painted side up and gently smooth in place. This will be the front.

Cut a hole in center of paper, then cut at 45-degree angles to corners.

Turn frame over. Apply a thin coat of glue to inside of back of frame and wrap paper through opening and over this section, trimming to fit and saving excess paper.

Cut paper at 45-degree angles from outside corners of frame. Repeat above procedure to glue paper to back of frame.

If any bare spots remain, tear a small piece from a scrap and glue in place, being careful to match color and texture.

Cut a piece of acetate to fit behind opening and glue to back of frame.

Position picture over acetate, and tape in place.

Cut a piece of cardboard for backing and glue in place.

Attach easel back or hanger.

Embellish front with conchos, nailheads, or other trims, as desired.

To lace edges, mark hole spacing on back edge of frame.

Place on wood work surface and drill hole around all 4 edges of frame with $1/8$-inch bit. Wrap a small piece of tape around end of lacing, and whipstitch around frame. Tie ends in knot.

HOW TO WIRE A LAMP

Wiring a lamp may seem like a formidable task, but once you understand the process, not only will you be able to repair a lamp, you will be able to make one.

A lamp can be made out of almost any jar or vase; the process for wiring any lamp is basically the same. Once you decide on the base, have a $1/2$-inch diameter hole drilled through the bottom of the vase or jar, and fit a length of $1/2$-inch diameter threaded metal tube into place. The length of the tube should be about $1/2$ inch longer than the height of the jar, letting just enough protrude to attach the base of the socket. (For example, a 10-inch jar will require $10^1/2$ inches of tube.) If you wish, you can extend the tube through the bottom of the jar and attach it with a nut to a brass base which can be purchased at an electrical supply or hardware store. If the jar or vase is stable and will later be filled with sand, shells, or other objects, the base may not be necessary. Use your own judgment.

A kit containing all necessary supplies for making a lamp can be bought at an electrical supply or hardware store. The only additional tool you should need is a screwdriver. Assemble the lamp parts as shown in illustration. (An underwriters' knot, the location of which is shown in second illustration, is enlarged in first illustration.)

Once your lamp is completely assembled, plug it in and check that it is working properly. Then carefully add the filler material of your choice to the jar or vase.

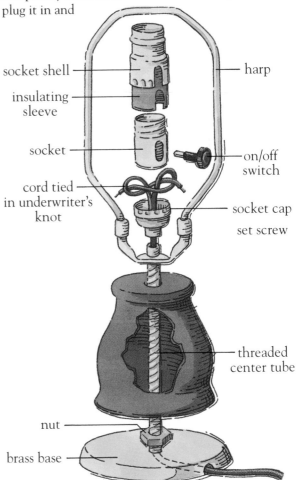

socket shell

insulating sleeve

socket

cord tied in underwriter's knot

harp

on/off switch

socket cap set screw

threaded center tube

nut

brass base

Once this is dry, the next step is to add stencilled details. The purchased stencil we chose provided designs that would set off the top of the doors and also work for our floor border. Refer to directions on How to Stencil, page 84.

The last touch was to paint the door pulls a bright yellow.

BUNNY FIREPLACE SCREEN

The warmth of a fireplace in the winter months can suddenly become a decorating challenge during the spring and summer. We believe this fireplace screen is just the solution for livening up the area. We used a bunny grazing in a wildflower meadow for our motif, but you can use any design that will coordinate with your nursery decor.

MATERIALS

1/4-inch plywood
Acrylic paints
Paintbrushes
Jigsaw or scroll saw
Router
Sandpaper
Clear varnish
All-purpose glue
C-clamps

ANTIQUED AND STENCILLED WARDROBE

A piece of furniture as prominent as this wardrobe is an excellent place to showcase painting details.

The base coat for the wardrobe is applied as it was for the crib and rocker. Once the white paint was dry, we made a glaze by diluting some of the blue paint used in the crib mural, and we applied it with a technique known as dragging. You might want to practice the technique on a scrap of wood or masonite before using it on your furniture.

First paint the glaze over a section of the painted surface. Then use a thick dry brush to remove all but a trace of the glaze. A wallpaper brush works well for large areas. Continue over the entire surface, removing as much as needed to get desired result. If you want to further soften the remaining color, you can use a dry cloth to gently wipe in the same direction of the brushstrokes.

DIRECTIONS

Determine screen size. (The finished size of our bunny screen was 20-by-20-inches.)

Enlarge design of choice to size, and paint on plywood. Let dry.

Cut out around design with saw. Cut two 3-by-8-inch triangles to serve as footed supports for screen. Rout 1¹/₂-inch groove in top center of triangle to hold screen upright.

Sand all rough edges. Paint triangle feet, edges and back of screen with a solid coordinating color of paint. Let dry.

Paint design as desired.

Seal all painted surfaces with 2 to 3 coats of varnish. Let dry between coats.

Place a line of glue in triangle grooves, and insert screen. Clamp together until glue is dry.

SHEER CRIB DRAPE

Softly flowing fabric frames the head of this crib, and echoes the poufed curtains and billowy clouds on the ceiling. Since it's not sewn, it can easily be untied and washed and then quickly put back up.

MATERIALS

Old microphone stand or similar stand
Crib
Pipe brackets
4¹/₂ yards sheer white fabric
Rubber band

DIRECTIONS

Position stand behind head of crib. Attach stand to back of crib with pipe brackets, using as many as needed to make stand secure.

Fold fabric in half as many times as necessary to make it right length to puddle on floor from top of stand.

Tie a large knot on one end of fabric. Wrap a rubber band around fabric just past knot. Slip rubber-banded area over stand and attach to top of stand with rubber band. Hide rubber band with folds of knot.

Arrange fabric around stand and crib, hiding all raw edges.

PAINTED CRIB AND ROCKER

Lovingly decorating a nursery is one of the joys of waiting for baby. It helps if you first determine a general theme and then use it as inspiration as you address each new project. This crib's end was painted with a scene that carries the room's theme of the idyllic outdoors. The rocker picks up the garden flowers in its fluffy, purchased cushions.

Before painting the crib and rocker, the old finishes were prepared using a liquid deglosser. The crib and rocker were then painted with 2 or 3 coats of high gloss oil-based paint for a more durable finish. The mural on the crib end was then painted, using children's books for ideas. Then, once all paint was dry, both pieces were sealed with a clear varnish.

THE NURSERY

The use of breezy fabrics and whimsical touches of paint turn a once simple room into a French Country nursery which excites the eye. Mismatched but color-coordinated sheets work perfection as a jabot with rosettes, and their airy, flowery quality echoes the crib bed drape, which is actually suspended from a discarded microphone stand, completely hidden behind fabric which puddles on the floor.

A simple plywood firescreen and marbleized contact paper soften the fireplace, while nearby, delicately stenciled bows and ribbons add light and interest to the floor. Antiqued in just one coat, the wardrobe features this same stencil and adds a touch of greenery.

Blue skies and fluffy clouds are ideal for the nursery, since babies spend much of their time looking at the ceiling. And the little bird in flight above the mantel adds an air of magic and a feeling of unity to the whole room.

This nursery contained the appropriate furniture and was a bright, sunlit space. However, the dark wood tones and the light-colored walls needed a splash of color to provide visual interest.

M A K E O V E R

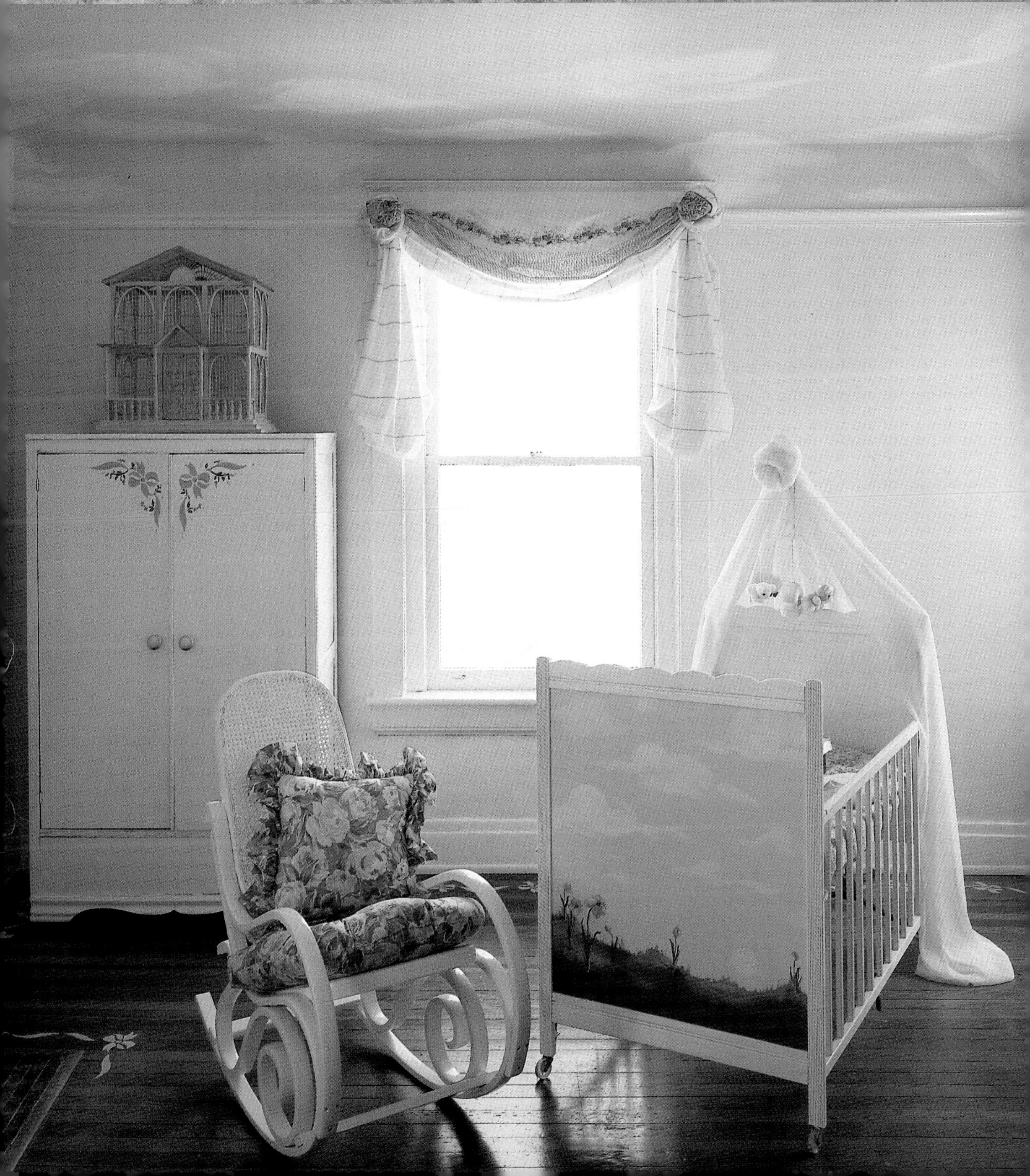

RECYCLED ACCENTS

Come over and raid the attic. That's the invitation Grandma issues when she wants to get the family together. She tells us she's getting rid of her old junk and to come over and find something we can fix up and use.

Grandma is a professional trash-to-treasure engineer, and she has passed her tricks of the trade along to me.

A discarded lamp shade becomes a conversation piece after covering it with a piece of bright fabric or paper. Need a shower curtain? Use a sheet! Punch holes carefully with the points of your scissors. Buy a liner for about a dollar at a discount store, and it's ready to go. Display your treasures, such as handmade doilies, intricately embroidered hankies, or even pictures, under glass on your end tables or dresser. Have a bunch of industrial-looking filing cabinets left over from the office? Take them to an auto body shop for an inexpensive coat of bright paint. If you have two, two-drawer cabinets, paint a discarded door to match and use it to top the cabinets as a desk. If the door is panelled, simply cover it with glass.

Convert a boring piece of furniture into a work of art with some colorful paint. Be liberal with your imagination—glue sequins or shells around a mirror or a picture frame. Or wipe an old wooden trunk with tung oil and use it for a coffee table.

Start with those pieces you've been avoiding in the garage, then attack your attic junk. And once you realize how easily and inexpensively trash converts to treasure, call your Grandma and ask if you can raid her attic too!

Easy paint techniques transform a few flowerpots and unused outdoor furniture into designer-look classics.

Instructions provided on pages 52–55.

Sponge-Painted Outdoor Furniture

If you have metal outdoor furniture that is ready for cosmetic help, don't repaint—sponge paint.

First, remove any peeling or flaking paint and loose rust accumulation with a wire brush. Then seal the metal with a rust-inhibiting metal primer.

Using enamel paints specially designed for metal, apply base coat if needed, and refer to directions on How to Sponge Paint, page 54. When all paint has dried, seal surfaces with 2 coats of exterior polyurethane sealer, allowing sealer to dry between coats.

Torchère Luminaries

Freestanding luminaries are wonderful. They let you decorate with light by moving the glow where it will be most effective. For a staggered grouping, cut the dowel sticks at varying heights.

MATERIALS

4-inch diameter terra-cotta flower pots
2-inch diameter terra-cotta flower pots
4 foot (1/2-inch diameter) wooden dowels
Wood saw
White primer
Paintbrushes
1-inch diameter fender washers
1 1/16-inch diameter fender washers
Spray enamel paint: yellow,
dark purple, lavender
Wood scraps
Old toothbrush or small stiff brush
Metal knife
Exterior polyurethane sealer
Wood scraps 4 inches square or larger
Plastic wrap
Patching plaster
#6 wood screws
Regular candles or citronella candles

A simple painted floorcloth and an inexpensive pinwheel unify a colorful patio grouping. Directions for these projects appear on pages 52–55 and 80–81.

DIRECTIONS FOR TORCHÈRE LUMINARIES

Each torchère has a 2-inch pot for candleholder and 4-inch pot for base.

Cut dowels desired height from ground to base of candleholder pot.

Paint dowels and flowerpots inside and out with white primer, and let dry.

Spray-paint insides of small pots and small washers yellow. Let dry. Apply a second coat if needed, and let dry.

Turn all pots upside down on wood scraps, and spray-paint pots and large washers purple. Let dry, apply second coat if needed, and let dry.

To spatter with lavender paint, refer to directions for tabletop luminaries on page 55.

When all paint is dry, apply 2 coats of polyurethane to pots and dowels, allowing sealer to dry between coats.

Wrap 4-inch scraps of wood with plastic wrap. Forming a thick paste, mix enough patching plaster to fill about 2/3 of each large pot. Place large pot on a wrapped wood scrap, and fill 2/3 full with plaster. (Plastic wrap will prevent wood scrap from sticking to pot.) Place other wrapped scrap on top of pot, and flip pot over. Insert dowel through drain hole on top and be sure dowel is straight. Hold in place until plaster sets enough to secure dowel. Allow plaster to dry overnight.

Wipe outside of pot with a clean, damp cloth.

Washers are used to give small pot stability. Place large washer on bottom of pot and small washer inside pot and position on dowel. Screw pot to dowel with wood screws. (If screws are not self-tapping, use nail or drill to form a pilot hole in center of dowel end before positioning washers and pot.)

HOW TO SPONGE PAINT

The painting technique of sponging is easy to execute with no special training. Before you tackle a project, try out the color and technique on a piece of plywood or sheetrock. (Ask at a lumber yard for a damaged piece).

Prepare the surface as you would for a regular paint job. Wash the surface to remove any residue and let dry.

Paint the project with a regular base coat of paint. Sponging involves thinning the second coat of paint and dabbing it lightly on the surface with a sponge. Use a natural sponge torn into a convenient size and shape. With gloved hands, dip the sponge in paint, then wring it out so that excess paint will not blob or run down the sponge-painted surface. Pounce (a light up-and-down motion) the sponge lightly and evenly on the wall, working in 3-foot-square areas and stepping back often to be sure the effect is even.

If you are working with more than one color, allow each coat to dry before proceeding. Be sure to rinse color from sponge and that sponge is thoroughly wrung out before proceeding, so that the next paint color is not thinned too much. Before applying successive colors to the surface, test each new color on a piece of paper to be sure it will match the previous series.

Turn torchère on its side, and seal plaster bottom with 2 coats of polyurethane, allowing it to dry between coats.

Turn right side up and insert candles. In mosquito season, substitute citronella candles for regular ones.

Helpful Hints: If washer prohibits candle from sitting squarely, use a bit of florist's clay or candle adhesive on bottom of candle.

Tabletop Luminaries

These outdoor luminaries draw their inspiration from the garden—they're painted flowerpots. The bright yellow inside the pots will pop with color during the day, then reflect a golden glow at night.

Materials

Medium-size terra-cotta flowerpots with saucers
White primer
Paintbrushes
Spray enamel paint: yellow, dark purple, lavender
Wood scraps
Old toothbrush
Metal knife
Exterior polyurethane sealer
Epoxy or super glue
Regular candles or citronella candles

Directions

Paint pots and saucers with white primer inside and out.

Spray-paint inside of pots yellow, and let dry. Apply a second coat if needed, and let dry.

Turn pots and saucers upside down on scraps of wood, and spray-paint outside purple. Let dry, and apply a second coat if needed.

Thin lavender paint slightly. Before spattering pots, practice technique on paper or wood scraps.

Dip toothbrush in paint. Sweep metal knife toward you across the bristles to create spatter. For larger spatters, knock toothbrush sharply against knife. Continue layering spatters over pots and saucers to get desired effect.

When paint is dry, apply 2 coats of polyurethane, allowing sealer to dry between coats.

Apply glue to bottom of flowerpots, and position on bottom center of saucers.

Insert candles. In mosquito season, substitute citronella candles for regular ones.

Painted Canvas Table Runner

Table runners allow you to add a strong design element to your table, using bolder colors and patterns than you might want over an entire tablecloth. This runner has those advantages plus one more—since it's painted and sealed canvas, it wipes clean for years of durable duty.

Materials

Cotton primed acid-free canvas
Acrylic paint
Paintbrushes
Masking tape
Clear polyurethane

THE DINING ROOM

This festive dining room beckons with warm colors and textures and has a surprisingly spacious feel.

With a few simple changes a South Sea Island theme emerges perfectly complementing the existing upholstery and china colors. Warmer terra cotta walls widen the dining area, while the deep tones in an easy marbleizing technique below the chair rail lend a gracious air of formality. A new light fixture is centered over the table, creating a new balance in the room.

Existing full-length sheers are folded over a long straight tree branch and knotted at the ends. Then a silk grapevine with dried beach grasses adorns the top of the treatment. This window treatment accentuates the tropical colors of the table runner and center-piece, echoing the South Pacific feel of this lovely decorating scheme.

A sparsely furnished dining room like this one is a decorator's dream with just a bit of time and creativity. The large triple-pane windows become a beautiful focal point for the room by bringing the outdoors inside. By changing the wall color, the room becomes visually larger.

Directions for Table Runner

Determine width and length that best suits table and cut out canvas, cutting ends in points if desired.

Work out design and color scheme on paper.

Lay down ground color, and allow paint to dry.

Sketch design on runner, using masking tape for straight lines.

Paint design.

Center of this runner was marbleized. Refer to directions on How to Create Faux Marble with Paint, below.

When design is finished and all paint has dried, apply 2 to 3 coats of polyurethane sealer, allowing sealer to dry between coats.

Helpful Hint: If finish wears with time, smooth out lightly with fine sandpaper, and add a fresh coat or 2 of polyurethane.

Basket of Antiqued Fruit and Silk Greenery

There's no reason to spend extra money for fancy latex fruit. You can transform inexpensive plastic fruit into beautiful antiqued pieces with a bit of glue and powder.

Materials
1 cup baby powder
Paper sack
Plastic fruit
Silk greenery
Spray adhesive
6-inch unwired pick
Green styrofoam block
Purchased basket
Spanish moss
Kiwi twigs

How to Create Faux Marble With Paint

You can marbleize almost any surface that you can paint. Marbleizing is easy, but the real joy of the marbleizing technique is that you can't mess up. You can smudge, sand, or paint out any area that does not please you.

For the base coat, select latex paint in a shade that will be the background color for the finished project. You will also need acrylic paint and marker pens in various colors to complete your design.

Place a puddle of latex paint in the center of a disposable pie tin. Place dime-sized drops of acrylic accent colors on either side of the latex

paint. Drag a 3 or 4-inch brush or sponge applicator through the palette, just tapping the edges of the brush or sponge in the accent colors. Test your strokes on a newspaper or plywood piece. Brush diagonally from left to right in a wavy motion. Repeat parallel strokes until the entire surface is covered.

While the paint is wet, use a finger or sponge to smudge any color that is too solid.

To add veins of pure color, dip the side of your brush or a feather in an accent color and apply it in a wavy line. Add accents of deeper color with a marker pen.

A marbleized mantel is the perfect backdrop for both silk lilac and ivy topiaries, with instructions on pages 59, 69, and 75.

DIRECTIONS FOR FRUIT BASKET

Place baby powder in paper sack.

Coat fruit and vines with spray adhesive.

Place a few pieces of fruit or vine at a time into bag and toss with powder to cover.

Remove fruit and vines from bag and let dry for at least 1 hour.

Insert 1 pick into the bottom of each piece of fruit. Insert styrofoam block into basket.

Line basket with moss.

Arrange fruit over greenery and insert picks into styrofoam block to hold fruit in place.

Randomly insert kiwi twigs into styrofoam.

MARBLEIZED MANTEL

Architectural details in a house offer many interesting places to feature painted techniques. This mantel is a perfect example. Begin by wiping down the surface with a liquid deglosser. This will allow paint to adhere well. Next apply a base coat of latex paint.

For a small area, you can use acrylic paints to marbleize panels in the fireplace and highlight carved details. Refer to directions on How to Create Faux Marble with Paint, page 58. We used a soft green for the majority of the mantel and mauve for the central panel.

When marbleizing is dry, use a small brush to paint details as desired. Once paint has dried, coat entire mantel with 2 coats of clear varnish, allowing varnish to dry between coats.

Spindle Candlesticks

Before you pitch out that old chair, take a good look at its legs. You might be looking at the perfect start for elegant candlesticks. Spindles from old furniture, banisters, peppermills—all sorts of turned wooden items—can take on new life with the right touch.

Materials

Wood scraps for tops or bases
Wood saw
Wooden spindles or turnings
Sandpaper
Wood glue
C-clamps
Black crackle medium
Paint brushes
White acrylic paint
Clear acrylic spray
Metallic gold paint
Wooden candle cups, if necessary

These candlesticks are crackle-painted to give an antiqued effect, while the bowl is marbelized with paint.

Directions

For pillar candlestick, cut a top and a base from wood scrap. (If spindle is sturdy enough to stand up by itself, a base piece will not be needed.) The base needs to be large enough to support spindle, and the top should be large enough to hold pillar candle.

Sand top and base pieces.

Sand wooden spindle to remove top layer of remaining paint or finish.

Glue top and base to wooden spindle using wood glue. Secure glued joints with C-clamps until dry.

Determine which sections of the wooden spindle will be painted gold.

Following manufacturer's instructions, apply black crackle medium to all portions of candlesticks that will not be painted gold.

Following manufacturer's instructions, paint white acrylic paint over black crackle medium. Allow to dry thoroughly.

Seal with clear acrylic spray.

Paint gold details, and allow to dry.

Seal with a second coat of clear acrylic spray.

For taper candlesticks, cut a base from scrap wood piece, if needed. Determine if spindle has an opening at top in which candle will fit.

If spindle hole will hold candle, proceed with sanding, assembling, and painting instructions for pillar candle.

If spindle does not have a hole or the candle will not fit hole, attach wooden candle cups to top of spindle with wood glue. Let dry, and proceed with sanding, assembling, and painting instructions for pillar candles.

MARBLEIZED WOODEN BOWL

If you have an old wooden bowl that has seen better days, revive it with a marbleized surface. Thoroughly wash and dry bowl to remove any remaining oils. When dry, coat bowl with primer. Refer to directions on How to Create Faux Marble with Paint, page 58. Finish with 2 or 3 coats of a clear sealer.

MARBLEIZED COLUMNS

The art of marbleizing turns attractive columns into a stunning frame for this richly-hued dining room. The tones in the paint repeat wall colors on each side of the columns, with golden accents added for spark and contrast. When choosing paint colors for an item that will be viewed from two directions, it's important to consider the effect each way and strike a balance.

To choose the proper type of paint, you need to know what type of paint you'll be working over. The old rule was not to use latex paint over oil-based paints, but new latex primers now make that possible. If you prefer the ease of latex but are not sure what you're covering, use a latex primer as a base coat to be on the safe side. And for interesting reflections when light strikes the surface, use a matte coat beneath a gloss marbleization, or vice versa.

Refer to directions on How to Create Faux Marble with Paint, page 58.

Gilded Napkin Rings

These sparkling napkin rings are an easy accent to make for the dinner table. Simple wooden napkin rings can be unearthed at garage sales and flea markets. You can create these in just a matter of a few minutes with a bit of gold paint and ribbon.

Materials

Wooden napkin rings
Fine sandpaper
Paper towels
Gold acrylic paint
1/2-inch wide gold wire-edge ribbon
Hot glue gun
Nailheads, buttons, or other baubles

Directions

Roughen surface of rings with sandpaper. Wipe clean with damp paper towel and let dry.

Wipe gold paint lightly over surface with paper towel, adding coats as needed to get desired effect.

Cut one 8-inch long piece of ribbon for each ring. Form small bows from each ribbon piece, and glue onto rings.

Hot glue nailheads with prongs bent in, buttons, or other baubles over center of bows.

Plaster Floral Container

To create this sculptural container, you begin with a plastic bowl and, like a child making mud pies, pack the plaster on roughly with your hands. The result is a piece that looks as if it could have been chiseled from stone. But remember that it's not. Plaster will crumble if banged sharply, so use care when handling.

Materials

Plastic container
100-grit sandpaper
3 pound box of hobby plaster
Disposable plastic container for mixing plaster
Disposable latex gloves
Electric hand sander
Stiff paintbrush
Acrylic paint: peach, white, gold
Clear acrylic spray

Directions

Thoroughly clean container to be covered with soap and water.

Roughen the plastic surface with sandpaper.

Follow manufacturer's directions to mix enough plaster to cover container. Wearing gloves, apply plaster over container leaving surface rough and textured. Allow to dry thoroughly.

Use electric sander to smooth the base of the container. Smooth high points on container with sander to achieve desired effect.

Use brush to dab on paint in a random pattern. Allow to dry.

Seal with acrylic spray.

Reupholstered Chair Seats

Chairs with drop-in seats like these are a snap to reupholster. In choosing fabric, there are several things to consider. Durable fabrics are especially important for chair seats, and if you choose an upholstery fabric with a rubberized backing you will not need to use cotton flannel sheeting between your fabric and foam. If your dining room gets direct sunlight, look for fade-resistant fabric.

Materials

Chair
Dense foam padding
Cotton flannel fabric
Upholstery fabric
Staple gun or finishing nails
Fabric protector, if desired

Directions

To determine fabric requirements for each chair, measure chair seat and add 3 inches to all 4 sides.

Remove seats from chairs.

Remove existing fabric.

Replace padding if needed with a dense foam padding. Cut new foam 1 inch larger than seat on all 4 sides so foam will completely fill seat area when fabric is pulled tight. Trim corners from top edges of foam if desired.

Place foam on seat bottom. Cover foam with cotton flannel fabric.

Cover cotton flannel with seat fabric.

A touch of gold brings new life to this dining room in a set of napkin rings, a plaster floral container, and reupholstered chair seats. For directions to make the flower arrangement see page 138.

Staple or tack fabric to bottom of seat in center of 1 side. Pull fabric in center of opposite side to bottom and secure. Repeat on sides, pulling and stapling in diagonal directions to keep fabric taut and smooth.

Trim excess fabric from corners.

Replace seat in chair.

Spray seat with fabric protector if desired.

BEDSIDE PICTURE FRAME

Convert an inexpensive tabletop picture frame into a coordinated bedside accent. Since all it takes is a bit of fabric, rope, and paint, you can use leftovers from a room makeover or just use up odds and ends from the scrap bag.

MATERIALS

Picture frame
Scraps of tulle or other gauze fabric
Masking tape
Hot glue gun
Scraps of 1/4-inch rope or cording
Acrylic paint
Paintbrush

DIRECTIONS

Remove backing and glass from frame.

Stretch tulle across frame front, and tape to back of frame.

Cut a diagonal line in tulle across picture opening. Stretch tulle to back of frame, making additional cuts as necessary to smooth fabric. Trim excess fabric, and tape in place. Hot glue tulle to back of frame.

Form designs on frame front with rope, and hot glue in place.

on How to Create Faux Marble with Paint on page 58. Finish with 2 or 3 coats of clear polyurethane or varnish.

STONE-LOOK FLOWERPOTS

Basic terra-cotta pots take on a whole new look with a bit of quick sponging. Seal the pot with a clear sealer before painting if pot will hold moist soil. Leave some of the terra-cotta color exposed and keep paint colors close in value to produce an antiqued quality.

Refer to directions on How to Sponge Paint, page 54.

FABRIC-COVERED OTTOMAN

Covering odds and ends with fabric can turn a mishmash into a coordinated suite of furniture. This ottoman is a good example. The skirt is a paisley polished cotton that picks up all the colors in the room. Use this same technique to make the fabric-covered bedside table, pictured on page 124, using a print design double-flat sheet for the main skirt, and muslin fabric for the overlay. Use straight pins to create the puffed skirt and stuff with batting if desired.

Paint frame and let dry. Apply additional coats of paint if desired.

Reassemble frame parts with picture.

Helpful Hint: Find images in magazines or use postcards for variety in framed pictures. Just trim the image to the desired size with a craft knife and metal straightedge, attach to a piece of paper or lightweight board with spray adhesive, and place inside frame.

MARBLEIZED COFFEE TABLE

If you have an old coffee table that needs refinishing, marbleizing might be just the thing. And to save time, you might want to refinish or paint the lower part of the table a solid color and only marbleize the top, creating the effect of a stone-topped table.

Lightly sand the surface before beginning, and wipe clean with a tack cloth. Follow directions

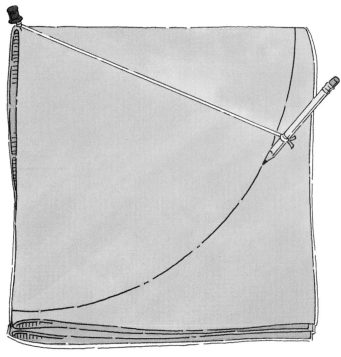

MATERIALS

Small round ottoman
Non-stretch string
Pencil
Paisley polished cotton
Straight pins
Cording to match fabric

DIRECTIONS

To determine the measurement for the fabric needed, measure the diameter of the ottoman top plus twice the distance from the top edge to the floor. Add 4 inches for puddling on the floor.

Make a compass by tying a non-stretch string around a pencil. To determine the length of the string, divide the sum of the ottoman measurements in half (top measurement, plus twice the distance from the top edge to the floor, plus the 4 inches for puddling, divided by 2).

These two pieces of furniture are refurbished using fabric remnants, a staple gun, and hot glue. To reupholster your own pieces, see pages 64–66.

Fold fabric in half horizontally, then fold in half vertically. Tack the end of the compass string at the folded corner of the fabric.

Swing compass in a arch shape. Be sure to hold the pencil perpendicular to the fabric.

Cut through all four layers of fabric along the penciled line.

Drape over ottoman, folding ends under.

Note: To make beside table overlay, cut a circle of muslin for overlay, using same technique as for polished cotton, but measuring drop from table edge to two-thirds of the way to the floor. Arrange overlay on table. Turn ends under, and catch with pins to create puffed effect.

Tie with a length of cording. Fray ends for fringe. Hold cording in place by catching cording with straight pins on inside of overlay.

Recovered Armchair

Turn a mismatched armchair into a coordinated piece of furniture for your guest room with a bit of leftover fabric, a staple gun and hot glue.

Materials

Armchair
Fabric
Staple gun and staples
Coordinated braided edging
Hot glue gun
Tassels

Directions

Cut a piece of fabric slightly larger than front of chairback.

Center fabric piece over front of chairback. Staple at center of one side. Stretch fabric taut and staple at center of opposite side. Carefully work out from centers toward corners, keeping fabric taut and smooth. Repeat to cover chairback and seat. Trim fabric at edge of staples.

Hot glue braid over staples and seams, tucking braid ends under to finish.

Tack tassels to front of seat at legs.

Pillows from Old Linens

Bits of pretty lace, old handkerchiefs, and frilly doilies are the inspiration for these elegant boudoir pillows. Whether you have well-preserved pieces or just salvaged edgings, you can create one of these delicate accents with a minimum of stitches.

Materials for Fan-Shaped Pillow

Scrap of peach fabric
Round doily
Thread to match doily
Polyester stuffing

Directions

Center fabric over wrong side of doily, and fold both pieces in half with fabric to inside.

Align and pin doily edges, adjusting as needed if halves don't match exactly. Topstitch on right side along decorative edge, leaving an opening for stuffing.

Topstitch just inside first stitching line, leaving opening for stuffing.

Stuff firmly, and stitch both seams closed.

Trim fabric inside doily as close to outside stitching line as possible.

Materials for Lace Strip Pillow

Peach fabric
Lace strips
Thread to match
Polyester stuffing

Directions

Determine desired size of pillow. Add ½ inch to each dimension for seam allowance, and cut 2 pieces of fabric for pillow front and back.

Determine arrangement of lace pieces on 1 fabric piece, and miter ends of central lace pieces if desired.

To miter, fold lace in half lengthwise with wrong side out. Stitch at a 45-degree angle from folded edge to inside raw edge of strip. Trim excess fabric, and turn so that seam is centered on back.

Position lace pieces on front of 1 fabric piece, and topstitch in place.

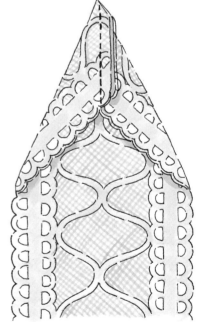

Place pillow front and back together with right sides facing and stitch with a 1/4-inch seam, leaving an opening for turning.

Turn, stuff firmly, and slip stitch closed.

MATERIALS FOR ENVELOPE PILLOW

Large monogrammed handkerchief
Muslin
Polyester stuffing
Thread to match
Peach embroidery floss
Tapestry needle

DIRECTIONS

Work with handkerchief to determine desired fold pattern.

Measure size of folded rectangle, and make a simple muslin pillow to fit inside.

Fold handkerchief sides over pillow and tack 1 in place.

Fold bottom up. Slip stitch sides of flaps and only tip of point in place.

Fold top down, and slip stitch sides of flaps in place, leaving point free.

Thread 12 strands of floss in tapestry needle, and thread through hem stitching of handkerchief.

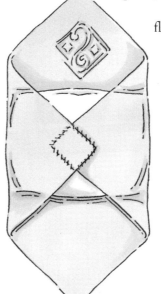

Here's a perfect solution for the family that outgrows an apartment; the dining area is converted into living space. Counter stools are cut down and used as a coffee table, while the counter itself conveniently serves as a couch table. A simple white sheet is tacked above the sliding glass door to lend an air of privacy.

COLORFUL SPHERES

Like bold dots of color, these decorative balls play off the shades used throughout this room. They can be displayed in a bowl, arranged on a mantel, or randomly spread along a table.

Best of all, they're so easy to make, you could enlist little hands in the effort, turning decorating into a family project.

MATERIALS

Masking tape
Craft foam balls in assorted sizes
1/8-inch thick jute rope
Straight pins
Craft glue
Glitter
Acrylic paints: brick red, purple, gold
Paintbrushes

DIRECTIONS

For "paper-covered" treatment, tear masking tape into strips and cover entire surface of ball with strips, smoothing wrinkles as flat as possible.

For rope treatment, wrap or coil scraps of rope around balls, securing with straight pins.

For glitter treatment, cover balls with glue and roll in glitter. Let dry.

Paint all balls in desired colors, and let dry.

LIBRARY COFFEE TABLE

If you need a coffee table but have an unusual library table, the answer to your problem might be right under your nose. Unless your library table is a valuable, pedigreed antique, it could make the change to coffee table in a flash—just remove the top, trim off the legs from the top to the correct height, and reattach the top.

MATERIALS

Library table
Right angle
Utility knife
Circular saw
Fine sandpaper
Tack cloth
Wood glue
Angle irons

DIRECTIONS

Determine finished height of coffee table. Measure thickness of table top and subtract that from height measurement to determine how much of the table legs need to be cut off. Use right angle to mark this measurement on legs.

Remove legs from table top. With a sharp utility knife, score marked line around all sides of all legs to help keep wood from splintering when cut.

Saw along scored lines, holding angle along lines to help guide saw if desired.

Sand cut edges lightly, and clean with tack cloth.

Run a bead of glue along cut edge of legs, position table top on legs, and attach with angle irons.

FLORAL BANDBOX

Here's a storage piece that is lovely to use in a grouping, whether for a tabletop, dresser, or window seat. And if your craft store doesn't carry bandboxes, try using an empty ice cream container or any cylindrical cardboard box with a lid.

MATERIALS

Scraps of wallpaper or wallpaper boarder
Cardboard bandbox
Ribbon to match

DIRECTIONS

Cut desired designs from wallpaper.

Carefully wet designs, and apply to bandbox.

Cut ribbon desired length for handle. Pierce bandbox, and insert ends of ribbon in hole. Knot to secure.

Repeat to attach ribbon to opposite side of box.

SILK LILAC TOPIARY

Silk flowers offer just about every imaginable hue, but pure white is still the classic choice. This lilac stem becomes a topiary when it's featured in a pretty clay pot and anchored with a bear grass arch.

MATERIALS

Green styrofoam block
Decorative clay pot
Craft glue
Spanish moss
1 (22-inch tall) silk lilac stem
Bunch of dried bear grass
1 (9-inch piece) silk ivy
Hot glue gun

DIRECTIONS

Cut foam to fit pot, and glue in place. Cover foam with moss.

Insert lilac stem in center of foam.

Insert bunch of bear grass at base of lilac stem.

Bend grass to form an arch beside lilac stem.

Tie bear grass in a loose knot at base of flowers, letting ends fall on opposite side of arch.

Hot glue ivy over Spanish moss at base of stem.

CRESTED THROW PILLOWS

Add some military polish to your sofa with crisp, crested pillows. Purchased emblems, navy and gold polished cotton, and gold cording combine to make three sensational accent pillows.

MATERIALS FOR 3 PILLOWS

3/4 yard (36-inch wide) navy polished cotton
3/8 yard (36-inch wide) gold polished cotton
Thread to match
Purchased emblems
Hot glue gun if needed
4 1/4 yards gold cording
12-inch pillow forms

DIRECTIONS

From navy fabric, cut three 12 1/2-inch squares and six 6 1/2-inch squares.

From gold fabric, cut six 6 1/2-inch squares.

Note: All seams are 1/4 inch.

With right sides facing, sew a gold and a navy square together on 1 side. Repeat.

Arrange 2 pieces so that colors will be diagonally opposite with right sides facing and sew 2 halves of pillow front together.

If emblems are iron-on, attach to front as desired following manufacturer's directions. Otherwise, hot glue in place.

Place pillow front on a large navy square with right sides facing and raw edges aligned.

Cut a 25-inch length of cording, and pin in place along pillow edge between front and back. Stitch front to back leaving an opening to turn and insert pillow form.

Turn, insert form, and slip stitch closed.

Repeat to make other pillows.

Gorgeous decorating accents, these covered and painted craft foam balls rival those found in designers' boutiques. The spheres provide a perfect compliment to the rich wood tones of an estate-sale library table, cut down to coffee table height. Create these stunning items with instructions on pages 68–69.

ROUND TABLECLOTH

Round tables covered with cloths are a decorating standard. Not only do they allow you to use fabric to add color and interest, they provide extra out-of-sight storage space.

To determine fabric yardage, measure the diameter of the table plus twice the drop (distance from the table edge to the floor), adding a little extra if you want the tablecloth to puddle.

The width of a double-wide sheet gives you enough fabric to cut a round, floor length tablecloth without seaming. Use a double flat sheet to make a cloth up to 81 inches in diameter, a queen flat sheet for 82 to 90 inches and a king flat sheet for a tablecloth 91 to 102 inches in diameter.

Fabric other than a sheet is usually not wide enough to make a round tablecloth without seaming, but you can sew two or three lengths of fabric together to create the desired width.

Make a compass by tying a non-stretch string around a pencil. To determine the length of the string, divide the sum of the table measurements in half (tabletop diameter measurement plus twice the drop and allowance for puddling, divided by 2).

Fold the fabric in half horizontally, then fold in half vertically. Tack the end of the compass string at the folded corner. Swing the compass in an arc, penciling a cutting line. Cut through all 4 layers of fabric along the penciled line.

Cording makes a very smooth finish for a hem. To determine how much cording you'll need, measure outside diameter of cloth. You can use purchased cording, or make your own from matching or coordinating fabric. If you're making your own, yardage will depend on width of cording, and most fabric stores have charts that will help you calculate this. Cut fabric in bias strips, piecing as needed to get desired length. Cover cord with fabric. Pin to tablecloth with cording on right side and all raw edges aligned. Stitch to cloth and press seam up in back.

Depending on where you plan to use the table, you might want to protect the cloth with a spray fabric protector or top the table with a piece of glass. To dress up the table for different seasons and occasions, use squares of coordinating fabric, lace, or handkerchiefs as overlays.

Plaid Couch Cushions

Don't give up on tired couch cushions. Give them a face-lift by covering the front with a bright new fabric. There are several alternatives for adding new pillow fronts, so you will need to evaluate your cushions to choose the technique that will work best.

Probably the easiest way is to cut a piece of fabric the size of the front plus ¼ inch all around, press the raw edges to the inside, trimming excess fabric from corners, and slipstitch over the old cushion. This is especially effective if you have cushions with cording to help hide the extra fabric thickness. But even if you have knife-edged pillows, you can use this technique and glue cording or braid over the seam to hide the extra thickness.

If you want to add a panel to your pillow front, you can cut a piece of fabric to the desired size and center it on the pillow front, basting it in place. You can then glue or stitch cording or braid over the raw edges.

If your cushions have knife edges and you want to keep them that way, you can just reconstruct the pillows. To do this, cut new front panels the same size as the old pillows plus ¼ inch for seam allowance on all sides. Gently slit the seams on old cushions, and set aside the best pieces to use for new pillow backs. Inspect the pillow forms or stuffing, and repair or replace as needed. With right sides facing, stitch new fronts to backs, leaving an opening for turning and inserting foam or stuffing. Turn, fill pillow, and slip stitch closed.

This updated den showcases ideal projects for working with what you have. Plain white paneling is dry-brushed in navy, inexpensive dried flowers are bundled and stacked, roadside weeds are spray painted and arranged, and the valances and sofa cushions are recovered. Update your own den with instructions on pages 20–21, 71–72, and 130.

ROOMY TUB TRAY

Here's a tub tray that will hold anything and everything you might want at your fingertips while bathing. And best of all, it started its life as a chairback, so there's no elaborate wood cutting involved. Just be sure to choose a flat chairback that is wider than the widest part of your tub, and the rest is smooth sailing.

MATERIALS

Wooden chair
Wood saw
Sandpaper
Enamel paint
Paintbrush

DIRECTIONS

Cut back from chair. Cut flush any arm or support joints. Sand smooth.

Paint with 2 to 3 coats of paint, letting chairback dry between coats.

STENCILLED AND PAINTED TUB

Clawfoot tubs are highly prized features in any bathroom. If you are lucky enough to have one, give it personality with easy stencilling and painting. The stencil chosen for this tub picks up the silk vines used elsewhere in the room, and the gilded feet repeat the room's brass and gold accents.

MATERIALS

White primer
Paintbrushes: wide flat, stencilling (1 for each color), small round
Masking tape
Purchased stencils
Stencilling paint in desired colors
Paper plate or saucer
Paper towels
Gold gilding paint
Clear varnish

DIRECTIONS

Paint outside of tub with white primer, and let dry.

Refer to directions on How to Stencil, page 84. Paint feet with gilding paint, and let dry. Seal tub and feet with 2 or 3 coats of varnish.

GOLD LEAF BOOKSTAND

One of life's greatest luxuries is soaking in a hot tub and turning the pages of an entertaining book. Here's a device that will help you keep the book dry while you soak. A simple plate stand, painted gold, will hold all but *War and Peace* with ease. For additional stability, glue or screw the stand to your tub tray.

MATERIALS

Fast-drying enamel paint, gold leaf
Paintbrush
Plate stand

DIRECTIONS

Apply 3 to 4 coats of enamel paint to surface of plate stand.

Let plate stand dry thoroughly between each coat of paint.

GOLD LEAF SHELL

Keep those sponges and soaps organized in a gift from the sea. This beautiful shell, painted gold, holds bathing odds and ends with style.

MATERIALS

Large shell
Fast-drying enamel paint, gold leaf
Paintbrush

DIRECTIONS

Turn shell open-side down, and apply 1 to 2 coats of paint to outside of shell.

Let shell dry thoroughly between each coat of paint.

LINEN BATHROOM ACCENT

Old linens are showing up all over the house these days, even in the bathroom. Here, a short table runner rests atop the tub tray, making a leisurely bath truly elegant. It would be equally effective on a chest or countertop. Doilies, lace napkins, and pieces of old tablecloths can provide a nice touch when hanging beneath hand towels or draped across the tank. The best approach is to pull out an armful and experiment.

IVY TOPIARY

Ivy topiaries are splendid by themselves or dressed up for special occasions. For weddings, they can wear bunches of white flowers. At Christmas, they can sparkle with small white lights. At Easter, they can sport some colored eggs. And the rest of the year, they can be enchanting stands of green.

MATERIALS

Purchased topiary form
Aqua spray paint
Rag
Green styrofoam block
Hot glue gun
8-inch basket
Silk ivy vines
Florist's wire

DIRECTIONS

For colored accents on topiary form, spray some aqua paint on rag and wipe over desired area. Let dry.

Cut styrofoam block to fit basket and insert into basket.

Hot glue styrofoam in place.

Fill basket with silk ivy.

Insert base of topiary form into middle of styrofoam block.

Wrap ivy vines around form and topiary ball until desired fullness is reached. Secure with pieces of wire if needed.

M I N U T E

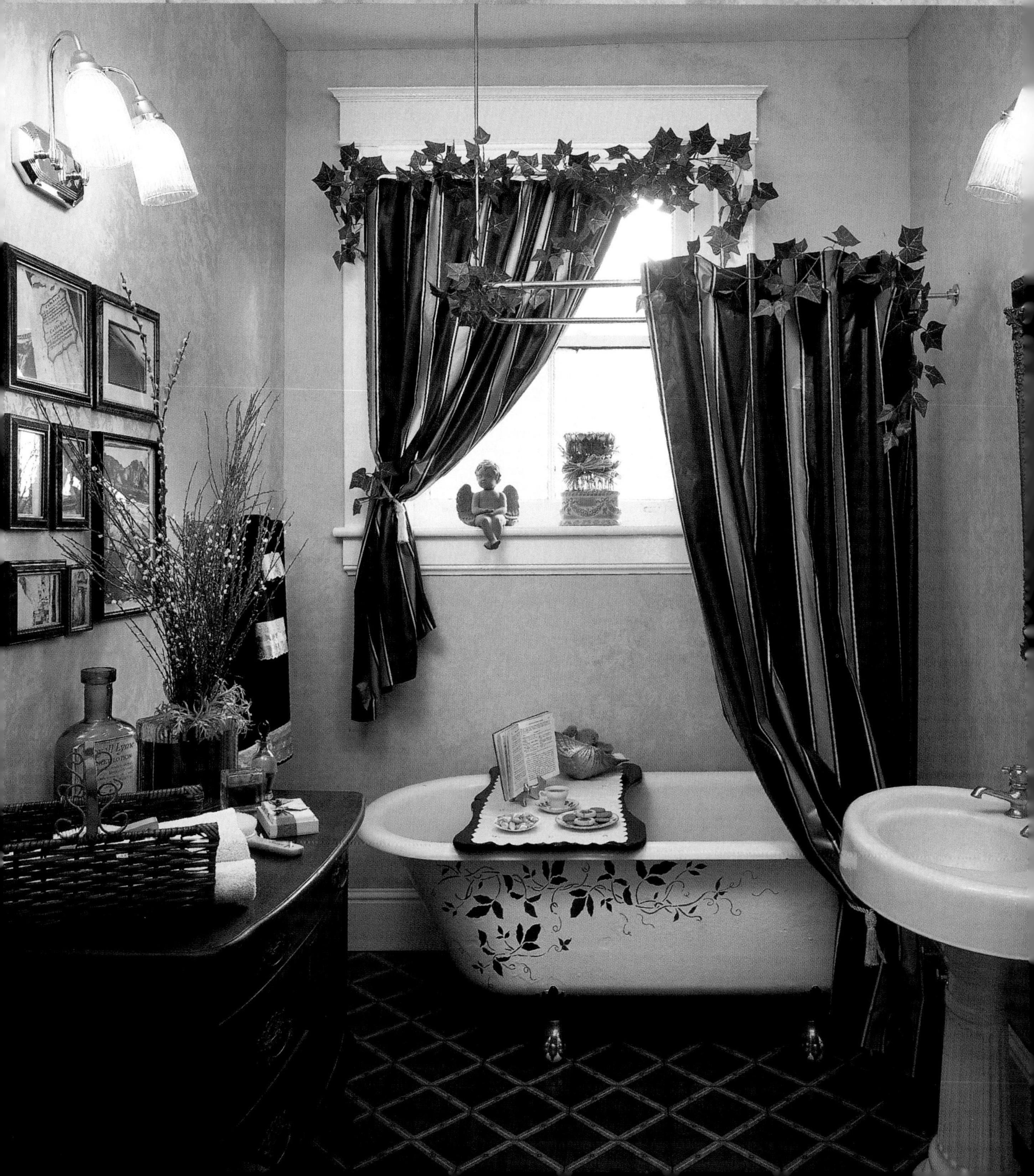

THE BATHROOM

This bathroom had much potential. Fine porcelain fixtures and a classic geometric floor pattern provided an unlimited number of possible choices for creating a truly enchanting room.

This bathroom is madeover to stimulate the eye while offering an invitation to soak and relax. Ragged tone-on-tone walls and rich polished cotton (under $4 a yard!) pick up the flooring colors, as silk ivy garlands and coordinated stencilling soften geometric lines.

Just a little touch of paint was used to bring out the detailing of the tub's clawfeet. A very enticing and oversized tub tray is crafted from the back of a discarded chair and filled with made-over items from around the house—an old plate stand becomes a book holder, a seashell transforms into a sponge container, and a linen table runner evolves into a bath accessory.

On the windowsill, a simple terra cotta cherub—available in lawn and garden centers—contributes to the classic theme of the bathroom. Full, no-sew curtains at the window and shower blend perfectly with the formal scheme.

The beautiful mirror above the sink is actually a yard sale find. It was a discarded picture frame that just needed a bit of dusting off and the addition of the mirror in order to become a showpiece.

On the dresser, a touch of green food coloring added to glass containers turns an average collection into a point of visual interest.

And a simple bouquet of pussy willow, Scotch broom, and fresh herbs is displayed in an old bottle, forming a delicate screen before the art grouping. The enlarged black and white photocopies of Italian architecture are mounted in inexpensive picture frames (about $2 each). The grouping echoes the Roman feel of this very alluring bathroom.

NO-FUSS FLOORS

Just what do you do with a naked floor? Once we'd ripped out our carpets, pulled up the staples, and cleaned up the mess, we stared hopelessly at our blank wood floors and wished for a genie with a magic lamp.

The living and dining room floors seemed so overpoweringly dark. So we lightened them with a pickling method which was surprisingly easy. We just thinned white enamel paint with mineral spirits, brushed it on, and then wiped away the excess with a clean cloth. For the den, our old sisal rug fit perfectly, but it needed some color. Since the carpet was divided into squares, we created a checkerboard pattern with black and white acrylic paints. Just a simple facelift, and our sisal rug looked fresh and new!

In the kitchen, we pulled up the vinyl and sanded off bits of glue, exposing the plywood subfloor. Rather than go to the expense of revinyling, we filled cracks, sanded them, then painted the kitchen floor ivory with an ivy stencil border. Paint also saved the day when our daughter wanted an expensive floral carpet she'd seen in a magazine. I bought some cotton canvas, hot-glued a 2-inch hem, stared intently at the magazine, and went to work with acrylic polymer paint and brush, sealing my paint job with three coats of polyurethane varnish.

After a few weekends and a little paint work, our whole house had come to life for only a tiny fraction of the cost of flooring or coverings. We didn't need a genie to create a house full of magic carpets!

Hiding the flaws in a plywood subfloor, a quick coat of sealed black paint is set off by a border of faux woodgraining.

To camouflage your own floor with these techniques, see pages 80 and 85–87.

PAINTED FLOOR

Whether you need to cover a plywood subfloor or mask flaws in your hardwood, sealed paint is more than beautiful and durable—it's inexpensive! Be imaginative if using this technique in children's rooms—try adding a hopscotch grid or a marble-playing ring before you seal your paint job. And for a more formal look after painting over hardwood, but *before* sealing, use a small routing tool to create a shallow, wall-to-wall groove between every third row of boards. This technique gives the illusion of wide, 19th century flooring.

MATERIALS

Putty knife
Fine-grit sandpaper
Oil-based primer
Flat oil-based paint
Paintbrush
Acrylic paint, if desired
2-inch masking tape, if desired
Clean cloths
Polyurethane

DIRECTIONS

Scrape away any remnants of grout, glue, vinyl, or other material from wood with putty knife.

Refer to directions on How to Refinish a Wood Floor, page 37.

Sand floor with fine sandpaper.

Apply 1 heavy coat of oil-based primer. Let dry.

Apply 2 coats of oil-based paint, letting paint dry overnight between coats.

To add a woodgrained inner border with painted side stripes, use masking tape to tape over area to be woodgrained, then add a strip of tape on either side of the first, exposing 3/4-inch floor areas for side stripes.

Use acrylic paint for side stripes, remove tape, and let dry overnight.

To woodgrain inner border, see pages 85–87 for woodgraining materials and directions, omitting steps 2 and 3.

Vacuum floor and dust with clean, slightly damp cloth.

Apply 3 coats polyurethane, letting dry overnight between coats.

PAINTED CANVAS FLOORCLOTH

While painted floorcloths were common even in Colonial days, today's materials and a wide variety of painting techniques make them better choices than ever for many rooms. They're an easy way to add color without spending a great deal of money and a fun way to practice some of those painted special effects such as marbleizing or ragging. And if floorcloths are sealed well, they can be cleaned and kept in good repair for years.

MATERIALS

Cotton primed acid-free canvas
Pinking shears, if desired
Acrylic paint
Paintbrushes
Clear polyurethane sealer

DIRECTIONS

Determine size, design, and color scheme. Cut out canvas, cutting short ends with pinking shears to suggest fringe, if desired.

Paint top side of canvas completely in a solid background color, and allow paint to dry.

Sketch design of your choice on canvas.

An inexpensive piece of canvas becomes a floorcloth, complemented by a watering can luminary and a burlap sack container. For more information, see pages 80, 81, 83, and 130.

WATERING CAN LUMINARY

If you have an old watering can that could be put to better use, think lighting. Here we've punched a design in the metal so that a votive candle's glow will filter out. On a porch or deck, it's both practical and part of the garden effect. We left ours natural, but you could add a spritz of paint if you want extra color.

MATERIALS

Old watering can
Wax crayon
Hammer
Nail
Votive candle and votive holder

Paint design.

Refer to directions on How to sections for instructions on painted special effects: marbleizing, page 58, sponging, page 54, and ragging, page 101.

When design is finished and all paint has dried, apply 2 to 3 coats of polyurethane sealer, allowing sealer to dry between coats.

If finish wears with time, smooth out lightly with fine-grade sandpaper, and add a fresh coat of polyurethane sealer.

DIRECTIONS FOR WATERING CAN LUMINARY

Lightly draw a design on can with crayon.

Fill can with water. If can has rust holes, seal them with melted wax so can will retain water.

Freeze water to create resistance for punching the holes.

Using hammer and nail, carefully punch small holes along outline of design. Allow ice to melt, remove wax if any was used, and finish as desired.

Insert votive candle and holder into can.

STENCILLED SISAL RUG

If you've priced these durable floor coverings, you know that sisal and coir rugs with designs on them can cost twice as much as the plain ones. They are such a good value that if you are even a little handy with a paintbrush, it's worth the effort to create a stunning rug in custom colors.

MATERIALS

Sisal or coir rug in desired size
Masking tape
Acrylic paints in desired colors
Medium flat paintbrush
Posterboard or manilla folders
Pushpins
Heavy cotton thread
**Stencilling brushes: ³/₄ to 1 inch in diameter,
1 for each color**

DIRECTIONS

Determine desired width of borders, and mask off with tape.

Paint borders, allowing rug's color to show through slightly. Let dry.

Note: If paint accidentally gets on wrong area of

Dynamic colors and repeated patterns rejuvenate a simple sisal rug. Patterns and instructions appear on this page.

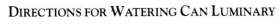

rug, blot immediately with a paper towel. If color remains, dilute with cool water and blot again.

Transfer patterns to posterboard or manilla folders, and cut out 1 stencil for each color.

Determine desired size of grid for design placement within border.

Insert pushpins at desired intervals along all 4 sides of rug. Run thread from pins on 1 side to pins directly opposite and tie securely. Repeat for remaining opposing sides to form grid with thread. Stencils will align, centered, on thread intersections.

Use a clean brush for each color, and test paint on a scrap of posterboard first.

Align stencil 1 on a corner intersection of grid, and paint using circular motion of brush. This will insure paint covers area beneath thread. Begin with a small bit of paint on brush, and build up color gradually to desired shade. Repeat at all thread intersections, and allow paint to dry.

Align stencil 2 on the next intersection of grid, and paint with circular motion. Repeat at other intersections to complete designs. Let dry.

Remove pushpins and thread.

STENCILLED NURSERY FLOOR

Purchased stencils provide the basis for this floor border. By taking the winding ribbon element from the stencils used elsewhere in the nursery, the floor design both enhances the overall decor and serves as a distinctive feature.

Since elements used as floor stencils tend to be simple, try using something from your upholstery or fabric—perhaps an interesting leaf or a geometric shape. Simply use thin paper and a pencil to trace the pattern, transfer the pattern to thin cardboard, and cut it out. Voila! You have a customized stencil to use on your floors!

Begin by carefully cleaning the area to be stencilled. Choose a paint compatible with the floor finish, then stencil following directions below.

Charming stencilled pink bows give a French Country look to this nursery floor. Refer to stencilling instructions below.

HOW TO STENCIL

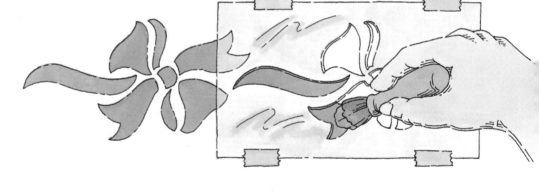

A little stencilling can add a stylish touch to walls, floors, and furniture. Books of precut stencils are readily available or you may want to create your own design. A good way to coordinate the stencilled pattern with the room's furnishings is to copy the design from fabric or wallpaper used in a room.

Once you've determined the design and are ready to begin to stencil, position the stencil on the surface to be painted. Use masking tape to hold stencil in place. Dip tip of brush into paint. Wipe off any excess paint on a paper towel until the brush appears dry and is light and smooth in appearance. Dab light layers of paint through the opening in the stencil working in a clockwise motion. Reverse direction and move brush in a counter-clockwise motion to build up paint to desired color. Continue to apply the paint until you have filled in all the design openings. Clean the front and back edges of the stencil frequently. When the paint is dry, apply a thin coat of clear acrylic spray to seal the design on the floor, wall, or furniture.

Broken Tile Floor

A cost-cutting flooring option, broken tile is perfect for small areas, such as hearths, half-baths, and mudrooms. Check with your tile retail store for local tile manufacturers, where availability of broken tiles will be at its best. (People in the tile industry call the broken pieces of tile "rubble," often pronounced with a long "u" sound.) Be sure to choose colors which will work well together, and to ensure that your floor will be level, only buy tiles that are the same in thickness. A two-gallon bucket of rubble will yield enough tile to cover a 10-to-15-square-foot area.

MATERIALS

1/4-inch substrate (pre-fab board), cut to size of area to be covered
Hammer
Penny nails
Thin-set
Notched trowel
Grout
Grout float
Clean sponge
Tile and grout cleaner
Rubber or latex gloves, if desired

DIRECTIONS

Remove any carpeting, nails, or staples. (It is not necessary to remove vinyl to lay tile.) Clean surface thoroughly and let dry.

Place substrate on area to be tiled and hammer to flooring with penny nails.

Spread a thin, even coat of thin-set on substrate with a notched trowel. Do not let dry.

Arrange tile as desired, leaving spaces in between to add grout later.

Let set overnight.

Mix grout according to manufacturer's instructions. Fill spaces between tiles with grout using a grout float, keeping grout-work level and even. Clean drops and messes as you go with a damp sponge.

Let set overnight.

Remove any excess film with tile and grout cleaner. Wear protective gloves if desired.

Woodgraining

The 150-year-old technique of woodgraining is perfect for masking unattractive surfaces, such as steel doors, particle-board shelving, or plywood flooring. When woodgraining over previously painted surfaces, be sure the area is clean and in sound condition, with no chipping or blistering. Here, we've woodgrained a faux oak border around a freshly painted bathroom floor to give the illusion of a hardwood inlay—this same technique looks just as lovely on a large desk, a heavy coffee table, or a level picture frame.

MATERIALS FOR WOODGRAINING

Medium-grit sandpaper
Spackling compound
Fine-grit sandpaper
Tack cloth
Masking tape
White primer paint
Paintbrushes
Gesso
Yellow Ocher acrylic paint
Alizarine Crimson tube watercolor
Goose quill
Acrylic paint
Polyurethane

DIRECTIONS

Before beginning this project, practice this faux-finish technique on a wood scrap to familiarize yourself with the technique and the use of the goose quill.

Sand area to be woodgrained using medium-grit sandpaper.

Fill any holes and dents with spackling compound, and let dry. Sand smooth with fine-grit sandpaper, and wipe with tack cloth.

If woodgraining only a border, use masking tape on both sides of area to be woodgrained.

Coat area with white primer. Let dry.

Coat area with gesso. Let dry.

HOW TO REFINISH A WOOD FLOOR

Refinishing a hardwood floor is a big job, but the results are worth it. Rent a drum sander and hand-held disc sander; be sure to ask for a demonstration before you leave the store.

Carefully check the floor and remove all staples, repair any loose floorboards, drive protruding nailheads below the surface, and fill any holes with wood putty. Vacuum and inspect the floor again. Now you are ready to begin sanding.

Start with 36-grit sandpaper. Tilt the drum up off the floor, grip handles tightly, turn on the power, and carefully lower sander to the floor, moving forward as you do. Work with the grain in slightly overlapping, parallel strips across the floor. Use the hand-sander with 36-grit paper for the edges and corners. Repeat the entire

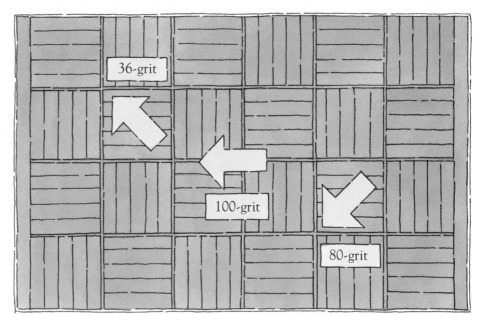

process with 80-grit paper. Check again for holes, then sand with 100-grit paper and vacuum again. Use the hand-sander with 100-grit paper at each end of the room to remove turn-marks. Vacuum the whole floor once more.

Wipe the floor with a tack cloth, then apply a clear sealer or stain. When dry, buff with fine steel wool and vacuum. Apply polyurethane or varnish and allow to dry at least two days. When the floor is completely dry, buff *lightly* with fine-grade steel wool and vacuum again. Seal with poly-urethane (which provides a no-wax, maintenance-free finish), and you're through. Or, apply two coats of paste wax and buff again with soft lamb's wool.

Note: If you are sanding a parquet floor, follow these directions, but sand in the pattern shown above.

Spatter-painting helps hide flaws.

WOODGRAINING DIRECTIONS CONTINUED

Paint area with two coats of Yellow Ocher acrylic paint and let dry after each coat. Squeeze a small dot of Alizarine Crimson watercolor onto area. Sprinkle a few drops of water onto paint dot to thin. Do not allow paint to become watery.

Brush mixture evenly over area, working with about a 1-foot strip or area at a time.

Drag edge of quill feather through paint mixture. The quill may be twisted, turned, or zigzagged through the paint to achieve desired results.

Continue technique until project is complete.

Remove masking tape if used.

If desired, border woodgrained area with a painted stripe as in photo on page 79.

Note: Do not apply masking tape over area that has been woodgrained.

SPATTER-PAINTING A FLOOR

If you have a scuffed wood or vinyl floor that you'd like to update without the replacement costs, try spattering it. In this carefree and easy painting technique, one or more paint colors are showered from a paintbrush to make spots that stand out against a solid background color. Depending on the colors you use and your individual spattering style, the result can be either bright or subtle.

MATERIALS

**White paint primer
Flat alkyd paint (for base color)
3-inch paintbrushes with squared-off
bristles (1 for each color)
Latex paints (for spattering)
Large sheets of white paper
Masking tape
Plastic sheeting, if desired
1   12-inch-long straightedge wood piece
Polyurethane
Mineral spirits**

DIRECTIONS

Paint floor using one coat of primer. Let dry.

Apply 1 to 2 coats of base coat, following manufacturer's directions. Let dry.

Note: Practice spattering on large sheets of paper before beginning project.

Thin latex paints with water, if necessary, to make paints consistency of milk.

Mask off baseboards and walls not to be spattered with masking tape and plastic sheeting.

Dip paintbrush into paint until bristle ends are filled with paint but not dripping. To spatter, hold straightedge wood piece about 1 foot from surface and tap metal part of brush handle sharply against edge of wood. (To make larger spatters, hold wood closer to surface and tap in same manner.)

Spatter entire floor with dominant color. Let dry.

Spatter with additional colors, if desired. Let dry.

Note: A darker color spattered over a lighter one gives a feeling of depth.

Apply 2 to 3 coats of polyurethane thinned with equal parts of mineral spirits to protect floor. Let floor dry thoroughly between coats.

CHECKERBOARD PICKLED FLOOR WITH BORDERS

This floor's checkerboard pattern is distinctive yet so subtle it doesn't overpower a light and airy room. The trick is to use diluted tints to stain the wood, creating a soft, aged effect. The added benefit is that the woodgrain of the floors is shown to advantage but in an unconventional way.

MATERIALS

Putty knife
Fine-grit sandpaper
Tack cloth
White oil-based primer
Mineral spirits
Masking tape
Paint tints: sagebrush and cumberland gray
Clean, dry cloths
Polyurethane

DIRECTIONS

Scrape away any remnants of grout, glue, vinyl, or other material from wood with putty knife.

(To strip a finished floor, refer to directions on How to Refinish a Wood Floor, page 86, but stop after wiping with tack cloth.)

Sand unfinished floor with fine sandpaper. Wipe clean with tack cloth.

Working in a 2-by-2-foot area at a time, wipe floor with 1 coat of white oil-based primer which has been thinned using 4 parts primer to 1 part mineral spirits. This will create a whitish, pickled look. Let dry.

Draw design on entire floor with a pencil, first drawing the border, and then the diagonal field of squares. (We used 12-inch squares, a 1/2-inch outer painted border, and a 3/4-inch inside painted border, leaving a 1-inch gap between the 2 borders.)

With masking tape, tape off all the squares that are to remain light, leaving the squares to be darkened exposed.

Wipe exposed squares with a tinted primer, using 4 parts primer to 1 part sagebrush tint. Gently wipe square with clean, dry cloth to achieve desired translucence. Let dry.

With masking tape, tape area on both sides of outside border.

An exquisite pickled checkerboard pattern has been wrapped in a double border and sealed with polyurethane. Directions appear on these pages.

Using the same sagebrush-tinted primer as for the darker squares, wipe masked-off area with primer-soaked rag. Wipe border to achieve desired translucence.

Remove tape and let dry.

With masking tape, tape area on both sides of inside border.

Wipe masked-off area with primer-soaked rag using 4 parts primer to 1 part cumberland gray tint. Gently wipe square with clean, dry rag to achieve desired translucence.

Remove tape. Let floor dry.

Apply 3 coats polyurethane, allowing floor to dry overnight between each coat.

EXTRA EASY WALLS

Walls do so much more than just hold up the ceiling. They're like a bare canvas awaiting an artist's touch. And you don't have to be Picasso to create wall decor that gives a room a new personality.

All it takes is a little time, a few cans of paint, and a feather duster. Feather dusting is one of the easiest painting methods around, and the finished walls look like they've been covered in expensive wallpaper. I've done it, so anyone can.

I always experiment on cardboard until I'm ready to start my walls. I use a darker base coat for a dramatic textured effect. A lighter base coat is best for creating subtle textures—but keep colors no more than two shades apart for that soft look. Once the base coat dries, dip just the tips of a feather duster into the second color. Tap it over the paint can to remove the excess paint, touch it to the wall, and pull it away. After I've covered a wall and let it dry, I often dust on a third color for more depth.

Beyond the feather duster, your cleaning closet is filled with perfect fabric "tools" for creating a wallpaper look, tee-shirts, cloth diapers, sponges, chamois, even rags! Pull an old piece of plywood out of the garage, twist your chosen tool into a rosette (or any shape to help you create a uniform pattern) and experiment with paints you already have—notice how easy it really is!

So maybe Picasso never dabbed paint on plywood with an old cloth diaper or feather duster, but I'm sure you'll be pleased with the results as you fill your own canvases with color.

This dramatic wall treatment is much easier than it looks and serves as an ideal backdrop for a sponged plaster end table.

The layered effect is created with stucco, white plaster, and sanded stencils. Instructions appear on pages 94–97.

Potato Print Stamps

Remember using potatoes to make stamps when you were a kid? The technique has stayed popular, and for good reason—it's easy, inexpensive, and fun! While we stamped a wall border and backs of canvas director's chairs, this technique works anywhere. Try glow-in-the-dark stars on a child's ceiling, subtle geometric shapes at chair-rail height in a dining room, or even ABCs randomly scattered across nursery dresser drawers. Just pull out some extra-large spuds, and adorn your home with bright color and graphic interest.

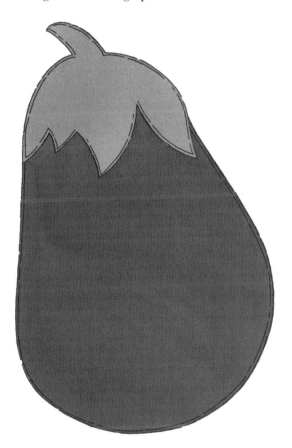

Colorful fruit and vegetable shapes are created with a potato-printing technique, just like in grade school! Easily constructed window valances are covered in canvas and striped in primary colors. And, with its naturally curled branches, a kiwi-twig arrangement helps to soften the hard angles of the room, as does a simple spray of backyard tulips. For more information, directions appear on pages 21–22, 93–94, and 128.

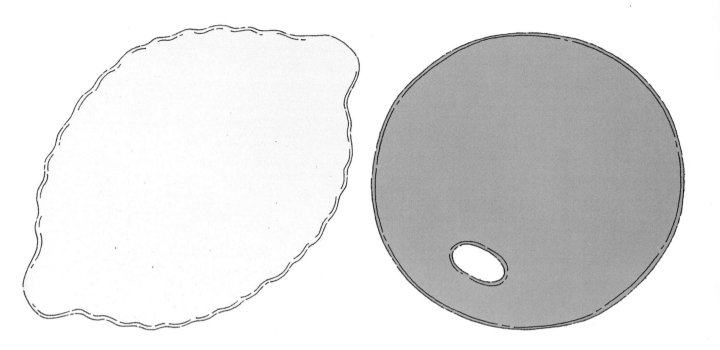

MATERIALS

Pencil
Dressmaker's chalk
Large baking potatoes
Long-bladed knife
Paring knife or craft knife
Acrylic paints
Paper plates
Paper towels
Stiff brush
Fabric protector for chairs
Pattern

DIRECTIONS

Use a pencil to lightly draw a line on wall where stamps will align. Determine desired spacing between shapes and mark on line.

Use dressmaker's chalk to mark chairbacks.

Cut a potato into halves using a long-bladed knife so that cut surfaces are smooth and flat. Wrap one half in plastic wrap to keep it fresh while working with remaining half.

Lightly score pattern outline on potato surface. Use craft knife or paring knife to cut out stamp shape. Cut away negative areas so that shape is raised 1/4 inch or more.

Practice stamping technique on paper before beginning on wall or chairs.

Spread a small amount of paint on paper plate. Blot potato on paper towel, dip in paint, blot lightly on towel, and stamp at first mark.

Repeat along line, leaving space for other designs between stamps of first design.

Repeat to cut and stamp additional designs.

When all paint is completely dry, erase pencil lines from wall, and use a stiff brush to remove dressmaker's chalk from chairbacks.

Spray chairbacks with fabric protector.

TEXTURED AND STENCILLED SUNROOM WALLS

Bestow beautiful rustic personality on a plain sunroom by covering the walls with texture and stenciling on bright geometric designs. This same technique can be used for an outdoor patio by changing the white plaster to white exterior latex and using exterior paint for stenciled designs. Just be sure not to sand through the paint to the stucco when you distress the designs.

Stucco exterior plaster
White plaster, lime base
Mortar trowel
Thin cardboard
Craft knife
Metal straightedge
Latex paint in desired colors
Stenciling brushes, 1 for each color
Coarse sandpaper

DIRECTIONS

Determine amount of stucco and plaster you'll need based on square footage of wall and manufacturer's guidelines.

Mix stucco exterior plaster according to manufacturer's directions. Apply to walls with mortar trowel, building up a layer $3/8$-inch thick. Let dry.

Mix white plaster according to manufacturer's directions. Apply a thin coat of white plaster over stucco with trowel until all plaster is concealed. Let dry, and leave coarse.

Mark stencil designs on cardboard. We used 3-inch squares and 3-by-3-by-$4^1/4$-inch triangles. Cut out with craft knife and straightedge leaving wide margins of cardboard around stencils.

Determine pattern arrangement and position on wall, and mark a guideline along area to be stenciled. Refer to directions on How to Stencil, page 84. Work with 1 color at a time, and allow each color to dry before stenciling next color.

When all paint is dry, sand stenciled area lightly to create a distressed, weathered appearance.

HOW TO PREPARE WALLS

Whether you re-wallpaper or try a paint technique, walls should be clean and smooth. New walls, repaired walls, or walls previously painted with regular latex paint should be sealed with an alkyd primer-sealer or a latex acrylic primer. Glossy enamel should be lightly sanded.

If the walls are covered with more than two layers of old wallpaper it must be removed. Use a utility knife to free an upper corner, and slowly pull the paper down. If paper won't strip off, it must be soaked with a commercial stripper or steamed off.

First, abrade the surface with extra coarse sandpaper. Wearing rubber gloves, carefully apply commercial stripping solution, following manufacturer's directions. After waiting the designated time, re-wet a small area and scrape with a wide scraper. Continue until all the wallpaper is removed, then scrub with a strong detergent.

For more stubborn paper, rent a steamer from a wallpaper store. Be sure to ask for a demonstration before you leave the store. Following directions, hold the steam plate to the wall as shown in illustration for two to three minutes, then scrape the softened section. Move the steamer to another section and repeat.

After all the old wallpaper has been removed, patch holes using patching plaster or spackling and let dry.

Sand walls smooth with very fine (200-grit or higher) sandpaper, and apply a coat of primer. The wall is now ready for wallpaper or a painted treatment.

BOW PICTURE HANGER

Hanging artwork from molding is a time-honored practice, but this fabric treatment gives it a fresh new look. The wire is concealed inside a gathered tube and the hanger itself is hidden under a crisp bow. The result is both practical and an effective way to repeat the look of the draped bed and tables.

MATERIALS

Unbleached cotton muslin
Thread to match
Picture wire
Picture hanging hardware

DIRECTIONS

Do not wash cotton muslin to retain its sizing and stiffness.

All seams are ¹/₂ inch.

Cut a 17-by-25-inch rectangle from muslin for bow. Fold in half lengthwise with right sides facing and sew along open long edge.

Turn tube right side out. Fold open ends together in middle and gather to form bow. Tack in place.

Cut a 6-by-12-inch rectangle from muslin for bow knot. Fold, stitch, and turn as for bow. Gather open ends and wrap knot around front of bow so that all raw ends are to the back. Stitch in place.

Determine desired length for gathered fabric that will conceal wire.

Double that measurement and cut a strip of muslin that length by 4 inches wide.

Fold in half lengthwise with right sides facing, stitch along open long edge, and turn. Insert picture wire and turn raw ends to inside.

Attach top of wire to nail or picture hanger, and other end to picture. Nail bow over top of tube.

SPONGED PLASTER FRAME ENDTABLE

Perfect for inside or out, this accent piece costs under $5 to make and will last a lifetime. Its base is a wooden frame covered with plaster that is antiqued, then painted. You can make any shape that will work with your decor. Squares and rectangles are easiest, but if you are comfortable shaping wood, you can get soft edges like those on our tree stump table.

MATERIALS

¹/₂-inch plywood
Jigsaw or scroll saw
³/₄-inch nails
Plaster wire, expanded, serrated edges
Mortar trowel
White plaster, lime base
Latex paint in desired colors
Sponges
Clear acrylic sealer

DIRECTIONS

Determine dimensions and shape of table. Cut plywood pieces to form base. For shaping wood, soak overnight in water, nail in place, and allow wood to dry thoroughly before continuing.

Wrap structure with plaster wire, shaping wire as desired and bending ends inward.

Mix plaster according to manufacturer's directions. Cover entire surface with plaster, filling out areas to desired shape. Let dry.

Place table outdoors and wet thoroughly with hose. Let dry. Continue wetting surface until desired amount of pitting in surface has been achieved. Let dry completely.

Refer to instructions on How to Sponge Paint, page 54. Seal with clear acrylic. Use 1 coat for indoor use or 3 coats for outdoor use, allowing sealer to dry thoroughly between coats.

Faux Marble Pedestal

This column pedestal looks as though it came from an old building, but it's really an inexpensive synthetic replica. Whether you have a plaster or synthetic column, you can create this effect.

Simply coat the column with a primer, then refer to directions on How to Create Faux Marble with Paint, page 58. Gray and cream colors were chosen to imitate real stone.

The capital of the column is painted black with a gilded band, then the column is finished with 2 coats of a clear polyurethane sealer.

Magnolia Art Drape

Whether you have access to fresh, fragrant magnolia blooms or you prefer the permanence of silk, this is a beautiful way to display flowers. Silk blooms can be attached by wrapping tape around the stems and attaching them to the frame back.

For fresh flowers, it's best to condition the cuttings before using them. Refer to the conditioning treatment on page 136 for details. Rinse any dust from the leaves and give them a quick wipe on top with a bit of vegetable oil for sheen. If you insert your magnolia cutting in florist's water vials, you can conceal the vials behind the frame or hide it under a large leaf. Use clear filament for extra support if needed.

By placing a pedestal underneath the artwork, we were able to draw the arrangement down below the frame, as well. For an unusual twist, we used a candlestick to hold this silk spray. A florist's water vial would be easy to conceal in the candlecup if using fresh flowers.

GOLD-TWINED FRUIT-AND-HERB BALLS

These little gems will probably end up everywhere in your house. We show them arranged on a table, but you could place a bowlful on a coffee table, or hang them with a velvet ribbon bow from the ends of a mantel, or the handles of a wardrobe.

MATERIALS

Hot glue gun
Dried apple slices
1   (3-inch diameter) styrofoam ball
1   (4-inch diameter) styrofoam ball
Bay leaves
#28 guage gold wire

DIRECTIONS

See Dried Fruit Slices instructions, page 17.
Hot glue apple slices over surface of balls, overlapping until balls are completely covered.
Hot glue bay leaves randomly over apple slices.
Wrap gold wire around balls. Tie off by inserting gold wire ends into foam balls.

BOTANICAL PRINTS

If you love botanical prints but don't love the price they fetch in galleries, here's an inexpensive alternative. Dover Publications offers a wide array of copyright-free images you can photocopy and tint. Their books are available in many craft outlets and can also be ordered through bookstores. The two books we chose our images from are *Handbook of Plant and Floral Ornament from Herbals* by Richard Chatton and *Early Floral Engravings of Emanuel Sweerts* edited by E.F. Bleiler. We used colored pencils to shade our images, but you might prefer to use watercolors or inks.

MATERIALS

Botanical images
Precut white mats with oval windows
Buff stock
Colored pencils
Acrylic paint: color to match prints, white
Paper plates or saucers
Stiff stencilling brush
Gold frames

DIRECTIONS

Choose copyright-free botanical images to use that will fit within the oval window of the mats, and photocopy them onto buff paper, reducing or enlarging as needed.
Shade the botanical images lightly with colored pencils.
Choose a deep shade of acrylic paint for mat color to accent colored prints. Squeeze a bit of undiluted paint onto 1 plate. Mix paint with white paint on another plate for a slightly lighter shade. Mix paint with more white on a third plate for a very pale shade.
Place mat on a flat surface. Beginning with medium shade of paint, hold stencil brush perpendicular to mat and punch brush onto mat surface. This technique is called stippling. Stipple over first coat with darkest shade of paint, and finish by stippling with lightest shade. Let dry.
Assemble prints, mats, and frames.

ALMOND BLOSSOM RAGGED WALLS

Here is illusion at its best. The effect of these paint colors, called pale almond and almond blossom, is that from a distance, the wall looks like stucco. The ragging technique suggests just enough texture to make large expanses of the wall interesting, while being soft enough to not overpower the pastel furnishings. And unlike stucco, it offers the advantage of wipe-down cleaning.

MATERIALS

Pale almond latex paint (for base coat)
Paintbrushes
Almond Blossom glazing liquid
Clean, dry rag

DIRECTIONS

Follow directions on How to Rag with Paint, page 101.

A simple drape of airy fabric delicately accented with wooden rosettes adds warmth and intimacy to these bedroom walls. Hand-tinted botanical prints with customized mats further enhance the tranquil feeling. See pages 98 and 100 for full instructions.

Architectural element
Wooden rosettes with mounting brackets
Fabric
Thumbtacks

DIRECTIONS

Determine position for architectural element centered above bed. Since this will be positioned over the head of the bed, be sure it is securely mounted to a wall stud. (If in doubt, hire a professional to install it—we did!)

Determine where rosettes should be positioned, and install them at each side of bed, following manufacturer's instructions. Refer to directions on How to Rag with Paint, page 101, if desired.

To determine fabric yardage, measure from the element to the rosette to the floor, add 8 inches, and double.

Fingerpleat fabric at center, and place on element, securing with a tack if needed.

Drape fabric over rosettes, arranging pleats as desired, and secure with tacks.

Arrange puddled fabric on the floor, concealing raw edges.

RAGGED BATHROOM WALL

Painted techniques can be subtle or bold, depending on how closely the different colors used are in tone. Here, we used two shades of gray latex paint that only vary slightly. We used the darkest color as the base coat, and then used a lighter glaze to create a soft, neutral effect.

MATERIALS

Latex paint (for base coat)
Paintbrushes
Latex paint (for glaze)
Clean, dry rag

DIRECTIONS

Follow directions on How to Rag with Paint, page 101. (Note: We used a cotton T-shirt as the rag in the bathroom.)

ROMANTIC BED DRAPE

In lieu of a headboard, try making this beautiful bed drape—it is a great place to show your originality. There are a wide array of architectural elements, old maritime parts from ships and docks, or other treasures that could make a striking focal point for the drape. And if you'd like to extend an expensive fabric, use a second, less expensive one in the same color layered underneath.

Art from Copied Images

You don't have to be a master photographer or spend a fortune at an art gallery to have a grand grouping of black-and-white images. Copy machines today produce a high quality of reproduction, and if you look, you'll find you have many sources for copies.

Begin with your own snapshot collection. Even color photos can often make interesting black and white copies, and by enlarging or reducing them, you can custom-size your image. Then look through the old family photo album, or take a trip to the local library. There are many visual books containing copyright-free images that can add to your choices.

The images we used here are all black-and-white in keeping with the decor of the room, but you might try tinting the copies with colored pencils, copying with buff-colored paper and brown ink, or experimenting with color copies. Even when you splurge for color copies, you'll still be spending far less than you would to have a photo reproduced by a photo lab. And once the art is framed and on the wall, you'll enjoy the variety this approach provides.

HOW TO RAG WITH PAINT

The tucks and creases of a bundled-up rag or a cloth design or the woven design of burlap or pieces of old lace can create interesting textured patterns when used in painting a surface. Ragging looks best on walls and ceilings where the distinctive patterns can be fully appreciated.

Before you tackle a wall, try out color and technique by painting on a large scrap of plywood or sheetrock. (Ask at a lumber yard for a damaged piece.)

Apply a regular base coat of paint. Once base coat is dry, apply an even layer of glaze to a small area, brushing thoroughly to even out the coverage. Glazing liquid has a syrupy consistency and can be colored with universal tints. Since glazing liquid is slow to dry, you can take your time working with it. (Note: You may use latex paint in lieu of glazing liquid, but apply it to a smaller area so that paint won't dry before you have a chance to finish.)

While the glaze is still wet, lightly roll a clean, lint-free, bundled-up rag in random directions until a pattern forms. Use a dabbing and pushing action with a slight twist for a clear design. Apply the glaze to the next patch and continue, allowing a small overlap pattern each time. Replace the rag when it starts to lose its effect. This job can be done by two people, one painting the glaze, the other using the rag. If the color dries too quickly, moisten it with a damp sponge.

Coordinated Art Grouping

With a little planning, you can take a collection of frames and images and turn them into a well-coordinated grouping. We began by looking over our unused frames and painting them all black. We then rounded out the collection with inexpensive frames we picked up at discount stores.

Instead of haphazardly placing nails in the wall and then deciding that the spacing is wrong, the correct way to determine the placement for an art grouping is to first lay the frames out on the floor and move them around until you have a pattern that works well together. (You may wish to use the black and white technique that we describe on page 101 for your photographs.)

If, after you go through this process, you have a few extras, you can use them on other walls to carry the theme throughout the room.

Mirror in Gilded Frame

Almost any attic we've ever seen has a few old pictures stuck away gathering dust. If the picture itself is neither loved nor valuable, take it out and reuse the frame. Even damaged frames can be called back into service. The mirror in this bathroom began life exactly that way.

MATERIALS
Frame
Tack cloth
Emery board or fine sandpaper
Spackle™ or acrylic modeling paste
Sawdust, if desired
Fast-dry gold leaf acrylic paint, if desired
Hot glue gun
Antique or new mirror, cut to size

This clever art grouping is composed of photocopied black and white architectural images. Placed atop an elegant ragged wall treatment, the grouping provides a lovely contrast to the delicate lines created by a pussy willow, Scotch broom, and fresh herb arrangement. For more details, see pages 101, 103, and 136.

DIRECTIONS
Thoroughly clean frame with damp cloth.

Lightly sand nicked places with an emery board or fine sandpaper. Clean with tack cloth.

Fill in any indentations with Spackle™ or acrylic modeling paste. For large repairs, mix sawdust with compound for better adhesion and strength. Let dry.

Lightly sand filled area. Clean with tack cloth.

Highlight raised areas on all sides with gold paint, if desired. Let dry.

Run a bead of hot glue around inside edges of frame and insert mirror into frame.

Scrunched Fabric Headboard

You may think you've seen everything that can be done with sheets, but we doubt it. By creating an architectural wall panel that coordinates with the room's windows, this headboard utilizes, you guessed it, sheets and unifies the various elements in the room, and at the same time it looks like a piece of fabric art. To make a coordinating fabric screen, use ready-made bifold doors hinged together. Once the fabric-covered cardboard is attached, cover the edges with painted wood lath or molding.

MATERIALS
1/4-inch plywood or melamine sheet
Decorative molding, cut to size
and painted
or stained
Wood glue
Finishing nails
4 metal joining strips and wood screws
Large piece of cardboard
Utility knife
Flat sheet, one size larger than bed size
Straight or T pins
Fabric stiffener
Paintbrush
Craft glue

DIRECTIONS

Measure width of bed and desired height of headboard from baseboard or floor to determine overall size.

Subtract from height the width of top molding and cut plywood or melamine this size.

Cut side molding pieces to fit on sides of plywood. Apply wood glue to back of molding pieces, and attach to side of plywood. Reinforce with finishing nails.

Position top molding on plywood, and attach with metal joining strips and wood screws.

Position headboard structure on wall and screw into studs in wall.

With utility knife, cut a piece of cardboard to fit within molding over plywood panel. (A large box opened flat will work, since fold lines won't show.)

Place cardboard on a flat surface, and position sheet on top of cardboard with top left sheet corner overlapping cardboard 1 inch on top and side. Pin in place.

Working from this corner, paint fabric stiffener on an area of sheet, saturating well. Scrunch fabric, being careful not to make folds too regular. Press low areas of fabric onto cardboard; pin to secure.

Continue process, applying fabric stiffener to no more than $1/4$ of the sheet at a time to prevent drying before fabric is arranged. Allow to dry overnight.

Trim excess fabric on edges to 1 inch all around, and wrap excess fabric to back of cardboard. Secure with craft glue, and let dry.

Remove pins from front of panel. Fit cardboard panel into recessed panel on headboard structure, and nail in place with finishing nails. Conceal nailheads in folds of fabric.

To keep bed properly aligned with headboard, mount bedframe to headboard with screws, washers, and bolts.

In this bedroom oasis, lilac walls are ragged in grape colored paint to bring out the deeper purples of the linens, and a coordinating king-size sheet provides texture variation when scrunched to cover a headboard constructed of plywood and white window molding. To use these ideas in your own bedroom, see pages 103, 105, and 107.

Lilac and Grape Ragged Walls

These walls show how strongly patterned a ragged technique can be. The base coat is a rich grape latex, and the ragging glaze is a clear, light lilac. When you are working with colors that contrast as strongly as this, your technique really needs to be precise—every smudge or repeat pattern will stand out—but the results are worth the extra care.

Materials

Grape latex paint (for base coat)
Paintbrushes
Lilac glazing liquid
Clean, dry rag

Directions

Follow directions on How to Rag with Paint, page 101. (Note: We used a cloth diaper as the rag in this bedroom.)

Navy Drybrush Wall Treatment

If you would like to tone down white or lightly finished wood paneling, this technique is both easy and attractive. Just choose a darker color to complement your decor—we used navy—and apply it with a dry brush. You might want to practice the technique on a wood scrap, or begin in an inconspicuous corner of the room until you get a feel for how much paint to load on the brush and how much pressure to use.

First, choose a paint that is compatible with the existing surface. Do not dilute paint. Dip a stiff brush in the paint—an old stiff brush on its last leg works great—and wipe excess paint on a paper towel. Stroke the brush along the surface so that

Accentuating the woodgrain, dry-brushed navy paint adds depth and visual interest to this painted paneling. This paint technique is explained at left.

the paint adheres to the wood grain and most of original color remains. Keep all strokes straight and going in the same direction, working with the grain. If you make a mistake, just wipe it off while paint is still wet, and repeat. This technique also works well on nubby fabrics such as heavy canvas.

Brightly ragged walls are a perfect backdrop for glimmering dried florals displayed in a simple-yet-stunning container crafted from dyed burlap and gold lamé. Wall treatment instructions are found above, while directions for the arrangement and its container appear on page 137.

THE GUEST ROOM

An invitingly classic air has been achieved in the formal guest room through the use of a lavish no-sew, two-fabric window treatment, easy staple-and-glued reupholstering, and innovative design techniques.

A once-discarded coffee table becomes a footboard accent piece, while a second table is marbleized and used below the window. The window's casement becomes a showcase for a distinctive madeover picture frame and sponge-painted flower-pots with moss topiaries.

Moss is also used at the footboard to cover an aging basket, edged in pine cones and filled with cedar and lavendar potpourri.

The room's balance shifts by relocating the bed and exchanging the heavy mirror above the mantel for a lighter portrait. Finishing off the makeover are stacks of old books, inexpensive art prints, and mismatched but complementary sheets, each creating visual interest while supporting the classic theme of this beautiful room.

The furniture placement in this room was a bit too predictable and the homeowner felt the room needed a facelift. The large picture window and distinctive fireplace and mantel are the cornerstones for creating what becomes an elegantly beautiful guest room.

ILLUSIONS OF SPACE

Space, the final frontier. There simply wasn't any the day we moved into our new house.

Boxes stood stacked to the ceiling in each small room. With very few closets and no garage, the frontier looked untamable.

But even the smallest home looks spacious if uncluttered, so our first task became organization.

We increased the storage space in our bedroom by turning an old library table into a mini-closet. Draping the sides and top of the table with a wide, heavy fabric remnant, I installed a heavy dowel on brackets underneath the table.

In the tiny master bath, we stored rolled towels in a wicker basket under the sink. And in a top corner of the shower stall, Bob hung a triangular net—the kind for holding stuffed toys—and we piled it full of washcloths, shampoos, and soaps.

For the children's rooms, we built under-the-bed storage units. We nailed plywood sheets to sawed-down skateboards, then we staple-gunned shoeboxes to their tops, leaving odd-sized gaps for hard-to-store items like baseball bats and rollerblades.

Since the den fireplace wasn't funtional, we thoroughly cleaned it and made a home for the TV which wouldn't use valuable floor space. We set the TV on an old wooden apple crate, turned open-side out to hold the VCR and tapes underneath.

In the kitchen, we painted a rickety ladder, hung it horizontally against the ceiling, and hung pots and pans from it.

With a little imagination, we faced our frontier and widened its horizons. So can you.

Taking its decorating theme from a cowboy comforter, this room's wall mural becomes three-dimensional by adding a simple canvas covered wagon canopy. Clever placement of a lasso-covered trash can and cork-covered screen give a lucky little cowpoke the feeling of riding the range. To tame your own frontier, instructions are found on pages 39, 40, 113, and 114.

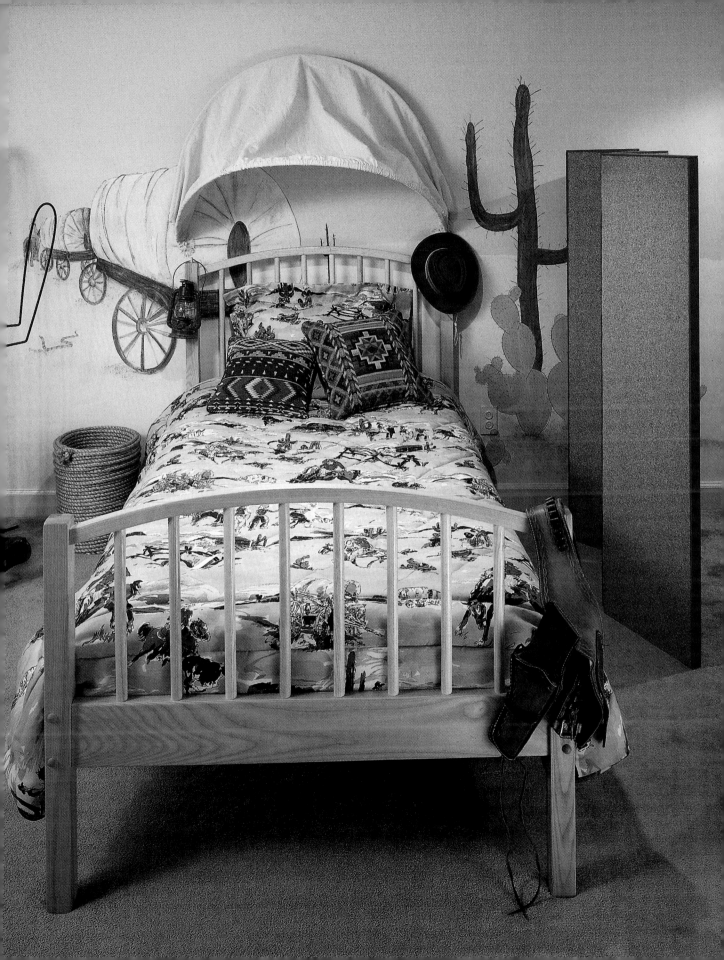

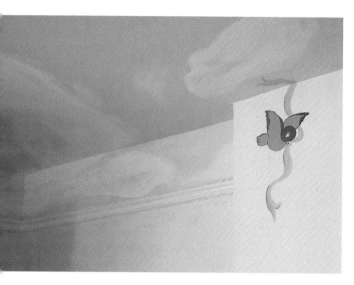

The great outdoors comes into the nursery with a little bluebird against a painted sky ceiling, accentuated by dropped crown molding. While the dropped molding would be enough to create a grand illusion of height, who can resist a blue sky filled with wispy clouds? Open up your own horizons with these decorating ideas.

HEAVENLY PAINTED CEILING

Let a canopy of clouds float above baby in your nursery. These billowy forms require more inspiration than skill. They seem to drift off into the heavens, lifting the ceiling right out of the room.

The dropped molding adds to the effect, and even if you have regular ceiling height crown molding, you might consider pulling it down the wall a few inches.

After you lay down the base coat of sky blue, just use a 2-inch paintbrush to form the clouds. Use round strokes, and feather the edges to avoid hard lines. Scatter the clouds irregularly, and make them different sizes to create a more realistic effect.

PAINTED BLUEBIRD ACCENT

What better place for the bluebird of happiness than in a nursery? The bluebird is adapted from a children's book design, whereas the ribbon comes from the stencil used on the wardrobe and floor. The placement of the ribbon gives the impression that the bird is carrying the ribbon back to its nest.

MATERIALS

Pencil
Acrylic paints: dark blue, light blue, yellow, pink
Masking tape
Paper plate or saucer
Stencilling brush: 3/8 inch to 1/2 inch in diameter
Paper towels

DIRECTIONS

Lightly sketch bluebird on wall with pencil.
Paint bluebird details using dark blue acrylic paint for outline, light blue paint for body, and yellow for beak.
Refer to directions on How to Stencil, page 84 for ribbon.
Add notched edges at ribbon ends.
Paint ribbon pink.
Shade ribbon edges with blue paint.

DROPPED WALLPAPER BORDER

If you have a room with high ceilings or just want to create a new visual point of interest, you can add the perception of depth by hanging a

wallpaper border that is dropped several inches from the ceiling. Wallpaper borders come in a wide range of styles, making it possible to match any decor. And by dropping the border, you can extend the ceiling color onto the wall above the border, creating both a softness at wall edges and a contrast with lower wall color.

To apply a border, begin by measuring and marking a line along walls for positioning. Cut lengths of paper to fit each section. Prepare the border according to manufacturer's directions, and roll it into a loop so that it's easier to handle. Position and brush out as for regular wallpaper, opening loops as you go.

CORK-COVERED FOLDING SCREEN

When are bulletin boards also room dividers? When they're found on a folding screen. This screen makes use of ready-made hollow doors, so construction time is reduced to a minimum.

HOW TO INSTALL A DIMMER SWITCH

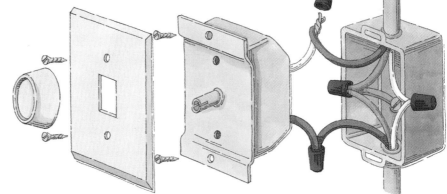

A dimmer switch, which can be installed on any incandescent light fixture, allows you to dim or brighten the lights in a room therefore enlarging or reducing the visual size at the turn of a knob.

Before you begin any electrical work, turn off the power to the circuit at the fuse box. Double check that the power is off by attempting to turn on both the light you are changing and the other lights in the room.

Unscrew the switch-plate screws and remove the switch-plate. Next,

unscrew the screws that hold the switch in the box. Gently pull the switch away from the box and disconnect the circuit wires by removing the plastic caps on the end of the wires. Straighten the wire ends coming from the box.

Connect the wires

from the box to the wires on the dimmer switch as shown above. To connect the wires, tightly twist the bare ends together and insert them in the plastic end caps. Twist the caps clockwise, making certain no bare wire is left exposed.

Carefully push the wires back into the box and screw the new switch into place. Finally, re-position the switch plate, screw it into place, and push the control knob onto the protruding end pin. Turn the power back on and enjoy.

MATERIALS FOR CORK-COVERED SCREEN

Roll of cork
2 sets of unfinished, hinged bifold hollow doors
2 extra hinges with screws
Fine sandpaper
Tack cloth
Wood glue
Trowel
Utility knife
Lath the same width as edges of doors
Wood saw
Paint in desired accent color
Finishing nails
Hinges

DIRECTIONS

Loosely roll cork in opposite direction, and secure. Let sit overnight to help flatten.

If doors are higher than desired screen height, cut to size. Remove spacers from scrap ends, and reinsert in cut bottoms to keep doors stable.

Sand doors lightly, and wipe clean with tack cloth.

Cut cork into pieces slightly larger than doors.

Lay doors on a flat surface. Spread wood glue evenly over top surfaces with trowel. Position cork on doors so that edges extend slightly all around, weight to keep flat, and let dry overnight.

Turn doors over, and trim excess cork with utility knife.

Repeat to attach cork to remaining sides.

Measure and cut lath to fit on top and sides. Paint, and let dry.

Nail lath on doors, and touch up nails with paint.

Attach hinges to form 4-panel screen.

TYPE TRAY SCREEN

You've probably seen type trays used for tables and wall display units, but here's a new twist. These trays are joined on back and hinged to make a screen. The texture they create is a striking accent that could work in just about any room.

MATERIALS

Old type trays
Metal joiner strips and wood screws
Hinges

DIRECTIONS

Note: Be sure to choose trays that are uniform in height, width, and depth. This screen uses nine 1½-by-16-by-32-inch trays to make a three-panel screen with 3 trays per panel. You can vary that layout to suit your space.

Remove handles from trays. For each panel, place short ends of trays together, and join with metal strips. Be sure screws go into tray frames for greatest stability.

Repeat to make additional panels.

Follow manufacturer's instructions to install hinges.

BUILT-IN WINDOW SEAT

You can create the feel of a master bedroom suite by building and installing a window seat. This bay was a natural place for a seat, but there are many places that can be transformed with a bench and cushions—a window between built-in shelves, dormers in an attic room, or windows at the end of a hallway. Once you start dreaming of a cushioned retreat, you'll probably be able to come up with just the right spot.

MATERIALS

¾-inch plywood
2-by-12 boards
2-by-4 boards
Circular saw or table saw
Wood screws
Drill with same size bit
Foam
Fabric
Craft glue
Staple gun and staples
1-inch wide (⅛ inch thick) wood lath
Hem tape
Finishing nails

This lovely type tray screen fills a vacant corner of the room and acts as a conversation piece. Unhemmed bolts of muslin are puddled and randomly draped over wooden curtain rods, bringing a classic feel to this eclectic living room. Instructions for the floral arrangement are on page 129, and type tray screen directions are on this page.

DIRECTIONS FOR BUILT-IN WINDOW SEAT

Determine size of bench: Measure desired depth from front to back and widths at front and back. Make a pattern of these measurements. Measure desired seat height, then subtract foam thickness and plywood thickness to get leg lengths.

Cut seat top from plywood.

Cut four 2-by-12 legs for back legs and front side legs.

Cut one 2-by-4 leg for center front leg.

Cut two 11³⁄4-inch squares from 2-by-12 board. Cut in half on diagonal to make 4 bracing triangles.

All legs will be inset 3 inches from edges of seat. Measure and mark leg positions on plywood. Bracing triangles will be positioned at a right angle in the center of 2-by-12 legs, forming a T. Measure and mark on plywood. Measure and mark positions for screws on all pieces. Drill pilot holes in all pieces.

front of seat and add ¹⁄2 yard for fullness. Cut fabric this size.

Press edges ¹⁄2 inch to wrong side. Secure 1 long edge with hem tape, following manufacturer's directions. (This is bottom of skirt.)

Cut a piece of lath the width of seat front at front legs. Position skirt on lath with top center of skirt aligned with top center of lath. Staple in place. Position edge of fabric so that it aligns with top of lath and extends 2 inches at each end. Staple one end and then the other. Arrange gathers between center and sides, stapling in place as you gather, or using pins to hold gathers in place as you staple.

Flip lath so that raw edges are to back. Use finishing nails to attach to front side legs and center front legs, hiding nails in folds.

Position seat in window, and top with pillows.

3"

2x12 backlegs

Bench seat top

3"

2x12 side leg

2x4 leg

2x12 side leg

3"

Center front

Brace

2x12 leg

Prop 1 end of seat securely, and align legs on other end. Attach top to front side legs and back legs. Position triangle braces, and attach to top and to legs. Repeat on other side. Attach front center leg last.

Using pattern for seat top, add ¹⁄2 inch all around, and cut foam for seat cushion. Add 9 inches all around, and cut fabric for cushion.

Use a dot of craft glue to attach foam to seat top at corners.

Position fabric centered over foam. Bring front center of fabric around to bottom of seat, turn raw edge under, and staple to seat bottom. Repeat on other 3 sides. Work in a diagonal pattern to continue wrapping and attaching cushion fabric.

For window seat skirt, measure drop from bottom of seat to floor, and add 4 inches. Measure width of

WINDOW SEAT CUSHIONS

With a dramatic treatment surrounding a window seat, solid tones are often the best choice for back cushions. Here, the large blue cushions pick out a dominant shade of the curtain and seat fabric and match piping on the bed's shams and throw pillows. But matching colors do more than coordinate different elements in the room. When color is used to break the flow of print from seat to curtain, it enhances the detailing of each.

BACK CUSHIONS

These are simple self-corded cushions, designed to fit the dimensions of the window seat. To make similar cushions for your space, begin by determining how high the cushions need to be to suit their function. We made ours as 20-inches square. Then decide whether you want a solid band along the back with cushion edges slightly overlapped, as we show here, or whether groupings in the corners would better suit your space. Finally, decide how the edges should be finished. Knife edges are, of course, the easiest, but with the array of purchased cordings, fringes, and weltings on the market, customized edges are easier than ever. These cushions were self-corded both to keep them a single color and to coordinate with bed coverings that have a similar cording.

TUCKED THROW PILLOWS

Interesting tucks and folds give these polished cotton pillows sophistication and style. The pillow covered with alternating squares takes the most time, but if you're looking for a short cut, how about using an old pleated skirt? If you don't have one you've been meaning to donate to charity, you can probably visit your local charity shop and find one that someone else did.

MATERIALS FOR ALTERNATING SQUARES PILLOW

1¼ yards rose polished cotton fabric
Thread to match
Polyester stuffing

DIRECTIONS

Note: Strips are oversize to allow for possible adjustment.

Cut a strip of fabric 18-by-24-inches long.

Starting 1½-inches from a short edge, make 14 (½-inch-deep) tucks spaced ½ inch apart. Press all tucks to the left.

Cut strip in half lengthwise to make 2 (9-inch-square) tucked pieces. Trim each piece to an 8-inch square, centering tucks on square.

Place squares together with right sides facing so that tucks on bottom piece are vertical and tucks on top are horizontal. Sew together along right edge with a ½-inch seam.

Repeat above procedure to make other half of pillow front. Place two strips together with right sides facing so that horizontal and vertical lines are arranged as pictured, and stitch together.

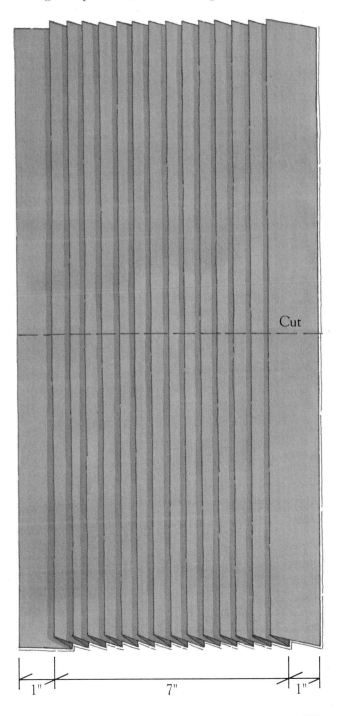

Cut

1"   7"   1"

Cut a same-size piece of fabric for backing. Place back piece on pillow front with right sides facing and stitch with a 1/2-inch seam, leaving an opening for turning.

Turn, stuff firmly, and slip stitch closed.

Finished pillow size is 14 inches.

Helpful Hint: Many prepleated fabrics are available in a wide range of colors. If you substitute one of these, adjust the finished size of pillow to conform with pleat size.

Cut a same-size piece of backing. With right sides facing, sew front and back together with a 1/2-inch seam, leaving an opening for turning.

Turn, stuff firmly, and slip stitch closed.

Finished pillow size is 13 inches.

MATERIALS FOR STRIPE TUCKED PILLOW

1 1/4 yard salmon polished cotton fabric
Thread to match
Polyester stuffing

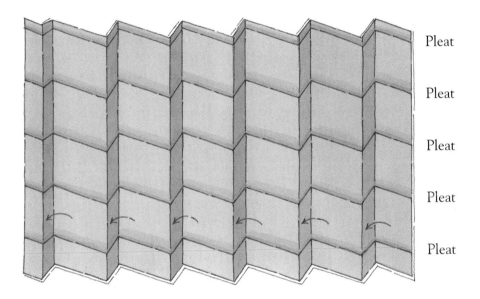

Pleat

Pleat

Pleat

Pleat

Pleat

MATERIALS FOR WINDOWPANE PILLOW

1 1/4 yard blue polished cotton fabric
Thread to match
Polyester stuffing

DIRECTIONS

Cut a 25-inch square from fabric. Beginning 1 1/2 inches from the left edge, make five 1-inch deep tucks, 3 inches apart. Press all tucks to the left.

Rotate strip a quarter turn clockwise. Repeat process to cross-tuck the tucked fabric and make a square pillow front. Trim seam allowances to 1/2 inch, centering tucks on square.

An ordinary bedroom is transformed into a charming suite with an inviting window seat, which also adds much-need storage underneath.

DIRECTIONS

Cut a 15-by-31 inch strip of fabric. Beginning 2 1/2 inches from left edge of strip, make two 1-inch deep tucks, 1 inch apart. Skip a 2-inch space and make 2 more 1-inch deep tucks, 1 inch apart. Repeat across pillow to make a total of 4 pairs of 1-inch tucks spaced 2 inches apart.

Press first 4 tucks to the left and the remaining 4 tucks to the right. Trim pillow to a 14-inch square, centering tucks on square.

Cut a same-size piece of fabric for backing. With right sides facing, stitch together with a 1/2-inch seam, leaving an opening for turning.

Turn, stuff firmly, and slip stitch closed.

Finished pillow size is 13 inches.

STENCILLED LAMPSHADE

If you like to stencil, you'll appreciate this quick way to customize a plain lampshade. A garland of ivy perfectly coordinates the shade and base.

MATERIALS

Purchased lampshade
Purchased stencil: ivy garland
Masking tape
Stencilling paint: hunter green, rose
Paper plate or saucer
Stencilling brushes: 3/8 inch to 1/2 inch in diameter, 1 brush for each color
Paper towels

DIRECTIONS

Place stencil in position and tape in place with masking tape.

Review paint manufacturer's instructions. Place a small amount of paint on a paper plate or saucer.

Dip tip of brush into paint. Wipe off excess on a paper towel until brush is "dry" and paint is light and smooth in appearance.

Hold brush perpendicular to surface. Start at outside edge of cut-out area and work in a clockwise motion from edge across design area.

Reverse to a counter-clockwise motion and continue building up color to desired shade.

Align print 2 if using more than 1 print, using register marks as a guide. Change to a clean brush. Stencil print 2. Continue stencilling until the design is complete.

Clean stencils and brushes gently following paint manufacturer's directions, and allow to air dry before using again.

Allow to dry thoroughly.

Attach lampshade to lamp.

A small basement provides plenty of growing room for little ones if you take advantage of wasted space. You'll be surprised to learn that raising the bed creates an additional twenty-four square feet of playing area. And this bright dinosaur wallpaper design creates enough visual activity to satisfy young creature enthusiasts.

By mounting mirrors to the long wall, the size of this master bedroom is visually doubled. And for rental property, a non-permanent equivalent can be made by mounting the mirrors to removable panels.

STACKED GLASS BLOCKS FLORAL DISPLAY

Glass blocks have made a real comeback in home design. They are readily available at most building supply stores and now come in more sizes and patterns to choose from than ever. These are stacked in an informal grouping to feature the top brick, which is really a vase. Filled with fresh silver-dollar eucalyptus, this is a freestanding arrangement of unusual loveliness.

To create your own glass block vase, just take the block to a glass company and ask them to cut an opening in one end to your specifications. Then use your imagination to combine a number of blocks in an arrangement beneath it.

RAISED SHEER CURTAIN

You can create the illusion of height at your windows simply by raising the top of the curtain to the ceiling. The result is a feeling that the entire ceiling has been lifted, especially when you use a light, sheer fabric.

MATERIALS
2 pegs
Sheer ecru fabric
Rubber bands
Cording

DIRECTIONS

Install pegs at top of wall directly above outside corners of window.

Measure distance from pegs to floor, add 1/2 yard, and cut fabric this length.

Gather and wrap corners on short end of fabric around pegs so that raw ends are concealed. Secure fabric around peg with rubber bands. Pouf fabric out at each peg.

Wrap cording around corner poufs and drape along folds at top of curtain.

Gather curtain to 1 side and tie with cording.

Be sure all raw edges are concealed in draping, and arrange puddle on floor.

DRAPED BED

Whether you are disguising a less-than-beautiful bed or are just wanting a light, fresh look, this draping technique is very effective. The vines add a dramatic touch and they're also easy to remove should you ever desire.

MATERIALS

64-inch wide muslin fabric
Safety pins
White cording
Honeysuckle vines

DIRECTIONS

Drape a width of fabric over headboard, working around curves and posts. Trim to fit, wrap raw ends of fabric to inside of headboard, and secure with safety pins.

Repeat at footboard, letting fabric puddle on the floor.

Wrap sides of bed, gathering fabric slightly, and secure on inside with safety pins.

Loosely wrap cording to cinch details on posts. Tie ends of cording in knots.

Refer to directions on How to Prepare Vines, page 129.

Wrap honeysuckle vines around posts and sides, draping across headboard if desired.

MARBLEIZED LOWER WALLS

Dining room walls often are divided by chair rails, and traditionally, one part of the wall is covered with wallpaper. If you are facing the decision of how to redo your walls, try marbleizing the lower section. It's less time consuming than doing a painted finish over the entire wall, and it can really anchor a room with rich, textured color.

We used rust as the base for this wall. We then worked up in lighter tones of the same color to get highlights. Finally, veining with feathers added just the right amount of detail.

MATERIALS

Rust-colored flat latex paint
Paintbrush
Dark, reddish brown acrylic paint
Sea sponge
Feather
Satin varnish

DIRECTIONS

Paint base coat on wall using rust paint. Let paint dry overnight.

Add several dots of dark, reddish brown acrylic paint to rust paint, stirring and adding more paint until a color a few shades darker than rust is achieved.

Using sea sponge, paint darker brown color over entire painted area of wall. Refer to directions on How to Sponge Paint, page 54.

Add additional dots of reddish brown acrylic paint to paint which has been sponged onto wall. Add enough additional acrylic paint to achieve a dark brown color.

Use feather to vein dark brown color over sponged wall. Let dry. Refer to directions on How to Create Faux Marble with Paint, page 58.

Paint a top coat of satin varnish over entire wall.

M I N U T E

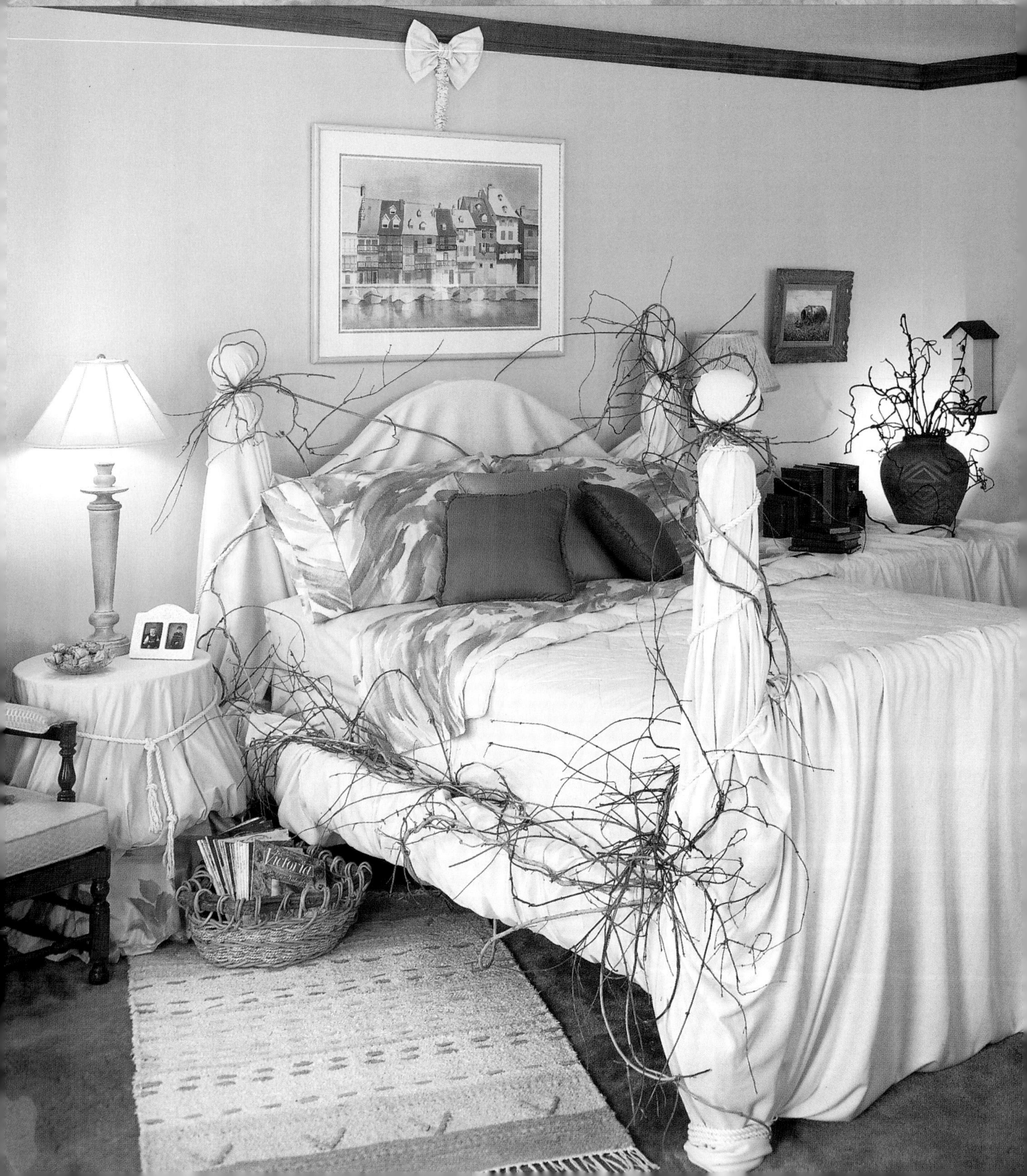

THE MASTER BEDROOM

A country-styled bedroom is transformed into this delightful retreat through the use of a common theme and color. The windows and madeover bed feature a layer of cream-colored curtain lining embellished with cotton cording. A wrap of honeysuckle vines around the bed frame creates the feeling of being outdoors.

This natural theme continues with the placement of a simple birdhouse above a sheet-covered bedside table and an arrangement of kiwi twigs in a clay urn. A clip-on reading lamp is mounted to the back of the bedside table, illuminating a darker corner of the room to give an illusion of space and depth.

Covering the second bedside table are twin-sized sheets, poufed and wound with more cotton cording.

The makeover is completed by the addition of an inexpensive art print, hung just above the bed and accented with a muslin bow and gathered runner.

This bedroom was nicely decorated, but the homeowner wished for a lighter, more natural bedroom retreat. The massive cannonball bed, pale walls and dark wood trim provided the perfect backdrop for a change in decorating style.

NATURAL ACCENTS

Every decorating magazine I read tells me to "bring the garden indoors."

Since I don't have time to keep a garden, I've learned to find and preserve natural accents for my own decorating. There are wonderful materials for arrangements available all year long right in your own neighborhood for free!

In the spring, break off or clip stems from flowering trees, and arrange them along the tops of your window treatments. Make a simple bouquet of greenery entwined with fresh blooming honeysuckle, and let the tendrils drape to the tabletop.

Late winter is the best time to find sturdy dried accents, perfect for spray painting, stippling, and even pickling. Take along clippers and rubber bands, and find a vacant lot or a nearby field. Look for dried plants with interesting leaves, seedpods, or blossoms. To make arranging easier later, keep plant types separated by bundling individual groups with rubber bands.

There are dozens of unusual yard and field items popular in floral design circles today. Used naturally or with a touch of paint, items include mosses, fuzzy weeds, wild onions, curly vines, empty wasp's nests, feathers, even abandoned birds' nests. These "finds" are sometimes arranged together, but more often placed individually within another fresh, dried, or silk arrangement.

Let your imagination run as wild as the weeds as you fill your home with nature's bounty. And as you discover more and more available natural accents, you'll realize that you don't have to be a gardener to bring the garden indoors!

A screen created from type trays becomes the perfect backdrop for this natural arrangement. Wild onion grass and twisted honeysuckle vines accent the focal point, a charming bird's nest. See page 129 for directions.

WILLOW BRANCHES IN BASKET

Curly willow forms a graceful, airy effect in arrangements. It's very useful in both fresh and dried arrangements, as you probably know if you like to arrange flowers. Between-times, store your branches in a large basket and let the winding stems work their magic alone. Here, we've placed it along-side a marbleized wall where the stems repeat the veining behind them, but they can be equally beautiful in most any room in your home.

KIWI TWIG ARRANGEMENT

Gnarled sticks are so dramatic that they can form stunning stand-alone arrangements. These kiwi twigs are a good example. Though you might have to go to the florist to find them and pay a little more than for a regular vine, you'll have a permanent arrangement that will be anything but run-of-the-mill.

Here we simply arranged them in a fan shape in a deep basket. For variety, use them in a tall narrow glass vase or with dried flowers in seasonal arrangements.

BIRD'S NEST IN THE BRUSH

Taking its cue from nature, this arrangement portrays a bird's nest tucked into the brush. Green onion grass provides the vertical screen, and looped and draping honeysuckle gives the arrangement texture.

MATERIALS

Green styrofoam block
Terra-cotta pot in stand
Craft glue
Sphagnum moss
Honeysuckle vine
Covered floral wire
4-inch wooden florist's picks
Purchased bird's nest
Wild onion grass

DIRECTIONS

Cut a piece of styrofoam to fit inside pot. Glue in place with craft glue. Cover styrofoam with moss.

Twist honeysuckle vine into a loop. Tie off with wire, wrapping ends of wire around a florist's pick. Insert honeysuckle in styrofoam.

Wire nest to a pick, position nest in center of vine loop, and secure to foam.

Attach a pick to a bunch of onion grass, and insert in foam behind nest and vine loop.

Insert a few pieces of honeysuckle vine at base of nest, and allow to cascade over pot.

GRAPEVINE VASE

Whether you need a large container for those budding branches in the spring or you have a spectacular dried arrangement that needs the right foundation, this vase is just the thing. Best of all, it makes use of a small plastic trash can—even if you don't have an old one to recycle, you can put together this great look for next to nothing.

MATERIALS

Small plastic trash can
Adhesive spray
Sand
Small grapevine wreath or loose grapevine
Hot glue gun
Acrylic spray paint

HOW TO PREPARE VINES

Vines are popular in today's decorating schemes, whether used for florals, window treatments, or wrapping furniture. They're beautiful used in their natural state and equally lovely if spray painted, stippled, or pickled. Most popular are grapevines and honeysuckle vines—both easy to find in your own yard or a nearby vacant lot or field.

Wear sturdy shoes, jeans, and a long-sleeved shirt to protect yourself, and take short and long pruning shears. Look for older vines, those that have entwined around one another to create a twisted effect. Clip the desired vine as close to the ground as possible, then find the other end or ends. Untangle the vine from its host plant, pruning the host only if necessary. Try to keep vines as long as possible so as not to limit your decorating possibilities.

Once you've gathered the vines, spread them out on the deck, patio, or lawn to strip them of their leaves. Do not strip the vines in long, swooping motions—this will remove the attractive tiny twigs and twists as well. Start at the top of the vine, and carefully pluck off any green growth, including leaves and green stems. Leave brown stems and curls intact.

Once vines are stripped, they are ready to use. If you plan to paint or pickle your vines, be sure that there is no moisture on the surface of the vines before you start. Let them dry in the sun if necessary. And if the vines become too dry before use, soak them in water overnight to restore flexibility.

When honeysuckle overruns your backyard, think decorating. Honeysuckle vines are a perfect natural accent to furniture, floral arrangements, even window treatments. See page 123 for instructions on how to dress up your bed.

DIRECTIONS FOR GRAPEVINE VASE

Spray sides of container with adhesive spray, and roll in sand. Let dry.

Carefully disassemble grapevine wreath or cut pieces of grapevine to size, and wrap around container. Hot glue in place.

Spray container with acrylic spray paint; let dry.

DRIED FLOWER TOPIARY

Rosebuds and other small, dried flowers crown this topiary. Choose flowers that match your color scheme to tie together elements in the room.

MATERIALS

Floral container
Green styrofoam block
Craft glue
Spanish moss
Small straight branch
Hot glue gun
4-inch diameter foam ball
Small dried flowers
Clear floral (spray) glaze

DIRECTIONS

For instructions on painting the stone-look container, see page 64.

Cut styrofoam to fit in bottom of container, and glue in place. Cover styrofoam with moss.

Insert stick in center of foam.

Put a dab of hot glue on end of stick, and carefully push foam ball onto stick. Cover ball with glue, and press moss over entire surface.

Hot glue dried flowers over moss, arranging in patterns and color groupings as desired.

Spray with clear glaze.

Arrange extra flowers over moss in container.

BUNDLED AND STACKED BROOM BLOOM

This totem of broom bloom forms an architectural element on a hearth. By changing colors and containers, you can take advantage of this sculptural effect in any setting.

MATERIALS

Green styrofoam block
Brass container
Craft glue
Spanish moss
Red dried broom bloom
Twist-ties, string, or wire
Hot glue gun

DIRECTIONS

Cut a piece of foam to fit in bottom of container, and glue in place.

Cover foam with moss.

Gather 3 equal bunches of broom bloom, and tie ends of each group tightly. Insert first bunch in foam.

Place hot glue on end of second bunch, and insert in middle of first bunch. Repeat to insert third bunch.

BURLAP SACK CONTAINER

Rustic materials used imaginatively really stand out, and this burlap container is a good example. It can hold anything from flowers to your knitting. If you plan to use it to hold a potted plant, use a water-tight container below the pot, and be careful not to overwater.

MATERIALS

Brown grocery bag
Burlap sack
Fabric stiffener
Paintbrush
Jute rope

DIRECTIONS

Place brown bag inside burlap sack. Fold down sides of sack to desired height.

Cover inside and out with fabric stiffener, following manufacturer's directions for use. Allow to dry thoroughly.

Wrap a length of rope around top just below fold and knot. Fringe ends.

Note: Burlap sacks can be found at coffee shops, hardware stores, and seed companies for as little as 25 cents.

Painted Dried Weeds

A weed by any other name would make a
wonderful dried flower arrangement. We wandered
along railroad tracks and fence rails to find the
materials for this bouquet of flowers.

Materials

Weeds
String
Spray paint: red, gold, blue
Green styrofoam block
Basket
Craft glue
Clear floral (spray) glaze

*Spray painted weeds and stacked broom bloom provide
the perfect finishing touch to this updated den.*

Directions

Gather weeds. Tie stems with string, and hang to
dry in a dark, warm place for 2 weeks.

Tie a line of string across room or between trees
on a still day. Tie materials to string line, grouping
by colors you intend to paint them. Paint desired
colors, leaving some natural.

Cut a piece of styrofoam to fit in bottom of
basket, and glue in place.

Starting with taller weeds in center, insert in
foam and arrange flowers in a circular, fan shape.

Spray with glaze.

Terra-Cotta Pot with Raffia and Floral Accents

Give a simple terra-cotta pot personality by covering it with a loose raffia net and embellishing it with dried herbs and flowers. Place a plastic saucer inside the pot so you can change out nursery pots of plants and flowers to suit the season and your mood.

MATERIALS

Natural raffia
Terra-cotta pot
Hot glue gun
Dried herbs and flowers

DIRECTIONS

Wrap a few lengths of raffia around neck of pot, and tie raffia in a knot.

Take several strands of raffia and holding them as one, slip over raffia around neck, leaving 2 equal lengths extending well past bottom of pot.

Continue at regular intervals around pot, spacing for desired size of netting.

Tie a length of raffia from one point to the nearest length at the next point in a knot, forming a triangle pattern. Secure to pot with hot glue under knot.

Beauty abounds in this lovely porch with the addition of touches from nature such as embellished terra cotta, curly willow branches, and a rag doll floral display. See pages 128, 132, and 134 for instructions on creating these lovely accent pieces.

Continue around pot until all lengths are tied and glued at the same level.

Repeat to form diamond pattern with next row.

Continue working down pot to form net pattern, tying as many rows as desired.

Wrap a few lengths of raffia around base of pot, and tie in a knot.

Tie off last row of net to raffia at base, and trim ends.

Embellish by gluing herbs and flowers onto pot as desired.

GRAPEVINE BIRDCAGE

Fashion a rustic birdcage to hang on the porch, in a sunroom, or in a breakfast room window. This is an easy decoration to make, but you might want to enlist the help of a friend to make weaving easier.

MATERIALS

16-inch diameter grapevine wreath
18-inch diameter grapevine wreath
Long strands of birch branches
Hot glue gun
Wire
Bird's nest
Purchased folk art wooden bird

DIRECTIONS

Smaller wreath will form cage top and larger wreath will form cage bottom.

Loop branches through bottom wreath and weave through top wreath, leaving a space between wreaths, referring to photograph.

Secure branches with hot glue if necessary.

When all sides have been formed, gather branches at top and tie together with wire. Trim ends even.

Glue nest and bird to bottom of cage, referring to photograph for placement.

Rag Doll Garden Party

This arrangement is perfect for last minute decorating. You just quickly assemble the elements, and then enjoy the results. And if flowers outgrow their space and need repotting, simply replace them with a new small pot of flowers.

Materials

Purchased twig sectional basket
Small pot of pansies
Small pot of geraniums
Small rag dolls

Directions

Choose a basket with each side section large enough to hold a 3- or 4-inch pot of flowers and a center area suitable for arranging dolls.

Place pots of flowers and their saucers on each side of basket.

Arrange rag dolls in center.

Conch Shell Centerpieces

Nature provides perfect floral containers in the many shells that wash up along the shorelines. The circular shapes of large scallop and clam shells lend themselves to low, rounded arrangements, while the assymetrical nature of the conch perfectly balances a fan-shaped design. While we've left our shells *au naturale*, you may want to sponge-paint yours before using them as centerpieces, either in the colors of your living room, or in gold or silver for a dining room. Refer to directions on How to Sponge Paint, page 54 for more details.

Materials

Green styrofoam block
2 large conch shells of same size
Craft glue
Spanish moss
Assorted silk and dried flowers and greenery
Clear floral (spray) glaze

Directions

Cut green styrofoam block in 2 pieces to fit snugly inside recesses of conch shells and secure with craft glue.

Hide styrofoam pieces from view by loosely arranging Spanish moss over them.

Begin arranging silk flowers and insert in foam, positioning to create focal point.

Insert tallest dried and silk materials behind silk flowers, and work down on sides to create a loose fan shape.

Fill in the spaces with shorter, fuller dried flowers or greenery.

Spray with clear glaze.

Place conch shell centerpieces on table.

Helpful hint: On a round table, this pair of conch shells would work best placed back to back, with their ends pointing in opposite directions. For a rectagonal or square table, refer to photograph for placement.

Seashell Mirror

If your summer vacations have left you with buckets of beachcombers' treasures, use them to embellish your accent pieces. Here, we've hot-glued shells in a pattern around an old mirror, but the technique looks just as lovely applied to a picture frame, bookends, or a medicine cabinet.

Materials

Assorted shells and coral
Large piece of paper to match size of mirror
Straightedge measuring device
Pencil
Mirror
Crayon or wax pencil, if desired
Medium-grade sandpaper
Tack cloth
Hot glue gun

Directions

Work on a large, flat surface, such as a floor or patio.

Sort shells and coral according to size and color.

Determine arrangement of shells and coral on large piece of paper, using straightedge for alignment. Once desired arrangement is achieved on paper, trace around shells with pencil. Make coordinating marks on mirror edges with crayon or wax pencil, if desired.

Lightly sand surface of mirror with medium-grade sandpaper to allow for better adhesion. Wipe clean with tack cloth.

Referring to paper for placement, begin at top of mirror, and hot glue shells and coral in place. Repeat until mirror is covered in shells and coral.

Helpful Hint: For the greatest visual interest, use shiny shells between matte-colored shells and make a central grouping at top of design.

If you have dining room furniture, but no dining room, think porch. A quick coat of white paint opens up the space, while a salvage store chandelier provides visual interest. Unifying the theme, small seashells are hot-glued around a yard sale mirror, while two large conch shells form the foundation for a striking centerpiece. To use these ideas in your own dining room, see pages 134 and 135.

Window Drape from Nature

If you like to take advantage of the gifts of nature in your decorating, here are a few tips to help. First, choose cuttings that will not leak sap. Take you cuttings early in the morning, and recut all stems under water to keep an air block from forming at the cut end.

Condition cuttings in a solution of 1 gallon water, 1 can or bottle of clear soft drink with sugar, and 1 tablespoon of liquid bleach for 24 hours before using. Decide how you want your cuttings to hang, and trim them to length. Insert ends in florists' water vials.

When hanging, conceal vials in folds of fabric, on back of curtain, or behind other blooms. Use clear filament if needed to secure your cuttings, and then enjoy!

Pussy Willow, Scotch Broom, and Herbs

Plants offer a great deal of variety in texture, color and size. The materials in this arrangement are an excellent example. In this vase, fresh pussy willow is a strong vertical dotted line. The budding Scotch broom is a greener, softer version of the dotted line effect. At the base, feathery herbs fringe the arrangement, giving it a finishing flourish.

MATERIALS

Glass vase or container
2 to 3 stalks pussy willow
Large bundle of Scotch broom
Fresh herbs of choice

DIRECTIONS

Fill container with water.
Insert Scotch broom into vase.
Insert pussy willow behind Scotch broom.
Insert herbs at front base of container.

PAINTED GRASSES AND FLOWERS

A stroll through a field can net you a dried arrangement that's a knockout. You may pick and dry the materials yourself or choose to purchase them ready to use.

MATERIALS

String
Dried grasses, flowers, and seedpods
2 purchased cornhusk flowers
Spray paint: gold, teal, purple
Floral container
Green styrofoam block
Craft glue
Spanish moss
Clear floral (spray) glaze

DIRECTIONS

String a line across a room or between trees on a still day. Tie materials at stem end to line, grouping by colors you intend to paint them.

Paint as desired, and let dry.

To make container, see Burlap-Wrapped Vase, this page.

Cut a piece of styrofoam to fit in bottom of container. Glue in place with craft glue.

Cover styrofoam with moss.

Begin arranging with cornhusk flowers. Insert in foam, positioning to create focal point.

Insert tallest dried materials into styrofoam behind cornhusk flowers, and work down on sides with shorter materials to create loose fan shape.

Spray with clear glaze.

Arrange extra flowers over moss in container.

BURLAP-WRAPPED VASE

Burlap's wonderful texture transforms a simple container into an eye-catcher. Here, we dyed the burlap deep purple and secured its folds with gold lamé, but the same materials can take on a totally different look with minor changes. Picture the burlap dyed a deep blue and wrapped with a strip of net embellished with small shells. Or imagine it dyed black and crisscrossed with jungle-print suede strips. Once you experiment with this concept, you'll see that it truly is a chameleon.

MATERIALS

Fabric dye in desired color
1 yard burlap or amount to cover container
Round trash can or similar container
Hot glue gun
Coordinating ribbon

DIRECTIONS

Dye burlap according to manufacturer's directions. Let dry.

Wrap burlap around container, folding and overlapping the material to achieve desired effect. Trim any excess fabric if needed.

Hot glue burlap at overlapping places and to container to secure.

Tie ribbon around top of container and knot to secure.

DESERT GARDEN IN A ROCK

This is a great way to introduce children to plants. Kids love spiky cacti and fleshy succulents, and these plants can withstand the seasonal droughts whether it's baseball season, soccer season, football season, or volleyball season.

Begin by enlisting your youngster on an archeological dig. You'll need to find an interesting rock with a deep enough hollow to hold soil and plants. Then, check with your garden center on selecting the proper soil and choosing plants that will not quickly outgrow your container and that also have the same light and watering requirements.

Once the two of you have tucked the plants into their new home, find a spot that gets the proper amount of sunlight, and discuss watering duties.

For directions on making container, see page 62.

Soak florist's foam in water until saturated. Wrap foam with tape in both directions to keep foam from crumbling when floral stems are inserted.

Cut stem ends at an angle underwater for easier insertion in foam and to keep air pockets from blocking stems.

Group roses in center of arrangement. Frame roses with long strands of spirea.

BUNNY AND LILY ARRANGEMENT

Silk blooms and a timid little pink bunny make a whimsical floral arrangement. From this magical garden plot, loosely cascading vines and flowering branches wind around a bunch of bulbs in a mossy field. Note: If you are unable to locate bunny pot like the one we used here, see Materials and Directions on opposite page for crafting your own.

MATERIALS

Bunny pot
Green styrofoam block
Glue
Sphagnum moss
Honeysuckle vines
White spray paint
Dry rag
Silk stargazer lily
Covered floral wire
Several stems of silk pink liptosporum
4 silk tulip bulbs

DIRECTIONS

Cut a piece of styrofoam to fit in large pot, and glue in place. Cover styrofoam with moss.

Spray honeysuckle vines with white paint and wipe with clean rag to create a pickled look. Let dry.

Insert lily in center of styrofoam.

Wrap 1 foot of honeysuckle vine in circle, and secure ends together with covered wire. Hot glue at base of lily, referring to photograph for placement.

Insert liptosporum into foam around lily as shown in photograph.

Glue tulip bulbs around base of lily.

Insert additional honeysuckle vines as desired.

ROSE AND BRIDAL WREATH SPIREA ARRANGEMENT

Fragrant fresh flowers, simply arranged, are hard to beat. The flowers chosen for this arrangement pick up shades of the container for a unified and refined effect. The best benefit of this arrangement is that its center roses are recyclable. Once the arrangement begins to fade, simply remove the roses, bundle their stems with a twist-tie, and hang them upside-down to dry. Soon they will form a beautiful dried rose bunch to use again and again.

MATERIALS

Floral container
Florist's foam
Floral tape
Fresh roses
Stems of bridal wreath spirea
Large twist-tie

MATERIALS FOR BUNNY POT

Pink spray paint
Clay pot for arrangement
Clay pot to hold bunny
Hot glue gun
Ceramic bunny

DIRECTIONS

Spray-paint both pots pink inside and out. Let dry.

Turn small pot onto its side and hot glue bunny to pot, referring to photograph.

Hot glue small pot to large pot on right side.

MOSS-COVERED TABLETOP TOPIARY

Bring a hint of the forest to your tabletop decorations. This moss-covered topiary is very effective grouped with objects similar in tone. It would also be effective with a partner on a mantel or windowsill or, if you make it low enough, on the dining room table.

HOW TO USE NATURAL ACCENTS

Decorating with natural accents is an easy and fun way to bring the beauty and vitality of nature into your home.

Whatever the season, think variety in texture, size, and color. In the spring, let soft-stemmed tulips cascade over the lip of a stoneware pitcher, group daffodils in clear vases of varying heights, float pansies in a tea cup, or place droopy hyacinths in a tall, narrow glass to support their heavy, fragrant beauty. And don't stop with flowers. Tuck early branches of forsythia or evergreens in your arrangements or wind into a wreath. Place pebbles and shells in a shallow dish, fill the dish with water, and float tiny blossoms in the pools.

Let the brilliant colors of summer guide your decorating in the hot months. Heap violets in a hand-painted china creamer, or arrange multi-colored dahlias in a variety of rough earthenware mugs and pitchers. When arranging summer flowers, remember to balance the warm colors of flowers with the cool greens of ferns, leaves, or moss-covered pebbles. Thistles, seedpods, or dried leaves make pretty additions to arrangements, as do rocks, twigs, and shells.

In the fall, take advantage of the variety of available fruits and vegetables. Surround a basket of freshly cut chrysanthemums with shiny red or yellow apples. Group gold and yellow marigolds with like-colored gourds.

Crystal vases filled with dried branches or seedpods can make a striking winter decoration. And old favorites like pine cones, sprayed gold or left natural, always add a nice decorating touch.

MATERIALS FOR MOSS-COVERED TOPIARY

Floral container
Green styrofoam block
Craft glue
Sphagnum sheet moss
Hot glue gun
Small straight branches
4-inch diameter foam ball
Tassel

DIRECTIONS

For directions on making container, see page 64.

Cut a piece of styrofoam to fit in bottom of pot, and glue in place.

Cover foam with moss, using hot glue to hold in place. Insert branches as a unit in center of foam.

Put a dot of hot glue on end of branches, and push ball onto them.

Attach moss to ball using hot glue.

Glue or tie tassel to base of topiary ball.

Here, a guestroom is accented with a basket bedecked with pine cones and moss and the topiaries lend a formal touch with their gold-embellished tassels and containers. Directions for these projects appear on pages 139–141.

MATERIALS FOR BASKET

**Basket
Brown fabric dye, if desired
Grapevines, if desired
Hot glue gun
Sheet sphagnum moss
Small pine cones**

DIRECTIONS

Antique a light, unfinished basket, if desired, by dipping it in a solution of brown fabric dye. Soak vines in hot water to soften if they are not freshly cut and pliable. Wrap vines around handle of basket and glue, if necessary, to inside of basket. Let dry.

Trim a piece of moss to fit an area of basket. Swirl hot glue on basket and press moss in place. Hot glue edges of moss to secure. Continue process to cover sides and bottom of basket, leaving rim uncovered.

Cover inside of basket with moss from just below rim to approximately 2 inches down sides.

Hot glue pine cones over rim of basket, also gluing adjoining pine cones together occasionally for stability.

Use small pieces of moss to fill in any gaps in pine cones and to cover any visible glue.

MATERIALS FOR POTPOURRI

**3$1/2$ cups cedar chips and shavings
$1/2$ cup lavender buds
Lavender and cedar essential oil, if desired
Bay leaves**

DIRECTIONS

Mix cedar and lavender together, adding a few drops of essential oil, if desired.

Arrange in moss basket, making sure some lavender buds are visible on top.

Scatter a few handfuls of bay leaves over top of potpourri, letting lavendar show through.

Add additional oil to refresh scent after it has faded, usually several months to a year later.

POTPOURRI-FILLED MOSS BASKET

Here's a lovely bit of woodland inspiration. An inexpensive basket is wrapped in rich sphagnum moss, topped with small pine cones, and filled with lavender buds and cedar chips. The beauty of the basket and the aroma it imparts greet houseguests with style. And if the fragrance begins to fade, drops of essential oils from time to time will revive it.

THE KITCHEN

A beautiful, airy work-space emerges from an old-fashioned kitchen with a minimum amount of effort. A fresh coat of warm color adds depth to wall areas, as the eye naturally wanders up to appreciate the stunningly simple window treatment and basket arrangement atop the cabinets.

In a variety of colors and shapes, baskets are placed along cabinet tops at varying angles, carefully avoiding predictably boring upright positions. Dried fruit slices backed with clothespins provide splashes of color, while objects placed inside the darkest baskets add a sense of depth and variety.

Nearly-sheer fabric allows sunlight through the room's focal point, a double-wide window, where a swag of honey-suckle vines, dried fruit slices, and herbs echoes the natural beauty found throughout this easy makeover.

Glossy white cabinets and a wooden countertop are perfect accents for creating a beautiful kitchen area, but this room needed a new coat of paint and some decorative accessories in order to create a truly homey feel.

HOME PORTFOLIO

Why wait till you can afford a designer when you can use Easy Decorating to beautify your home right now? Start developing your themes here in Home Portfolio. Pull out your paint chips, fabric swatches, magazine clippings, and "before" shots and attach them throughout this chapter. You'll enjoy having them conveniently in one place where you can adapt the ideas in this book to fit your home, as well as dream up all-new decorating ideas.

Home Portfolio also handles the business end of your decorating, featuring places to fill in your window dimensions, appliance manufacturers, floor square footage, building materials, and more. Once these vital statistics are in place, it becomes a breeze to plan your projects and shop for materials. And when you find a future need on sale, guesswork is eliminated because you'll have precise measurements and colors right in your hand!

This chapter is also designed to help you protect your home. In each room section, there is space to record the names, styles, and values of your furnishings. Clip an envelope of furnishing snapshots to the back of the chapter, and Home Portfolio becomes a handy tool for insurance records.

And most fun of all, we've included pages of furnishings and a grid so that you can play with your rooms without messing them up! Feel free to photocopy those pages and use them to design and redesign as you add to your home decor.

Clip on photos, tape on interesting magazine articles, affix sticky notes of ideas or sketches,

and staple on wallpaper or fabric swatches and paint chips.

L I V I N G

Have an interesting idea about your living room decor? Just jot it or sketch it on a sticky-note, and place it here till you have time to pursue the idea!

Are your end table drawers filled with swatches and paint chips? Tape them here and you'll always know the right shades or patterns for touch-ups or new accents.

Did you see something exciting in a magazine? Paper clip the photo, article, craft idea, or advertisement right here so you can keep it handy! (Be sure to check the magazine classified section for discount supply houses and their 60-75 percent savings!)

Has someone passed on names of talented and reasonably priced upholsterers or carpet cleaners? Tape their business cards and brochures here so that you can take bids whenever you need them.

Do you have "before" or "after" photos of your living room or shots of you and your family working on home projects? Glue them here so that they will become a part of your home portfolio.

R O O M

Floor

Dimensions _____

_____

Covering _____

_____

Windows

Dimensions _____

_____

_____

Style _____

_____

Fabrics _____

_____

_____

Walls

Dimensions _____

_____

_____

_____

Wallcovering _____

_____

_____

Paint _____

_____

_____

Trim

Style/Type _____

_____

_____

Stain/Paint _____

_____

_____

Built-ins

Dimensions _____

_____

_____

Stain/Paint _____

_____

_____

Furnishings

Name	Brand/Style	Value

D I N I N G

Have an interesting idea about your dining room decor? Just jot it or sketch it on a sticky-note, and place it here till you have time to pursue the idea!

Are your buffet drawers filled with swatches and paint chips? Tape them here and you'll always know the right shades or patterns for touch-ups or new accents.

Did you see something exciting in a magazine? Paper clip the photo, article, craft idea, or advertisement right here so you can keep it handy! (Be sure to check the magazine classified section for discount supply houses and their 60-75 percent savings!)

Has someone passed on names of talented and reasonably priced furniture refinishers or silversmiths? Tape their business cards and brochures here so that you can take bids whenever you need them.

Do you have "before" or "after" photos of your dining room or shots of you and your family working on home projects? Glue them here so that they will become a part of your home portfolio.

R O O M

Floor

Dimensions _____

_____

Covering _____

_____

Windows

Dimensions _____

_____

Style _____

_____

Fabrics _____

_____

_____

Walls

Dimensions _____

_____

_____

Wallcovering _____

_____

_____

Paint _____

_____

_____

Trim

Style/Type _____

_____

Stain/Paint _____

_____

_____

Built-ins

Dimensions _____

_____

_____

Stain/Paint _____

_____

_____

Furnishings

Name	Brand/Style	Value

Have an interesting idea about your family room decor? Just jot it or sketch it on a sticky-note and place it here till you have time to pursue the idea!

Are your desk drawers filled with swatches and paint chips? Tape them here and you'll always know the right shades or patterns for touch-ups or new accents.

Did you see something exciting in a magazine? Paper clip the photo, article, craft idea, or advertisement right here so you can keep it handy! (Be sure to check the magazine classified section for discount supply houses and their 60-75 percent savings!)

Has someone passed on names of talented and reasonably priced carpenters or slipcover makers? Tape their business cards and brochures here so that you can take bids whenever you need them.

Do you have "before" or "after" photos of your family room or shots of you and your family working on home projects? Glue them here so that they will become a part of your home portfolio.

R O O M

Floor

Dimensions _____

_____

Covering _____

_____

Windows

Dimensions _____

_____

_____

Style _____

_____

Fabrics _____

_____

_____

_____

Walls

Dimensions _____

_____

_____

_____

Wallcovering _____

_____

_____

Paint _____

_____

_____

Trim

Style/Type _____

_____

_____

Stain/Paint _____

_____

_____

Built-ins

Dimensions _____

_____

_____

Stain/Paint _____

_____

_____

Furnishings

Name	Brand/Style	Value

Have an interesting idea about your kitchen decor? Just jot it or sketch it on a sticky-note and place it here till you have time to pursue the idea!

Are your kitchen drawers filled with swatches and paint chips? Tape them here and you'll always know the right shades or patterns for touch-ups or new accents.

Did you see something exciting in a magazine? Paper clip the photo, article, craft idea, or advertisement right here so you can keep it handy! (Be sure to check the magazine classified section for discount supply houses and their 60-75 percent savings!)

Has someone passed on names of talented and reasonably priced cabinet makers or appliance repair people? Tape their business cards and brochures here so that you can take bids whenever you need them.

Do you have "before" or "after" photos of your kitchen or shots of you and your family working on home projects? Glue them here so that they will become a part of your home portfolio.

K I T C H E N

Floor

Dimensions _____

_____

Covering _____

_____

Windows

Dimensions _____

_____

Style _____

_____

Fabrics _____

_____

Walls

Dimensions _____

_____

_____

Wallcovering _____

_____

Paint _____

_____

Cabinetry

Dimensions _____

_____

_____

Stain/Paint _____

_____

_____

Counters

Dimensions _____

_____

Covering _____

_____

Trim

Style/Type _____

_____

Stain/Paint _____

_____

Appliances

Name	Manufacturer	Value

Furnishings

Name	Brand/Style	Value

MASTER

Have an interesting idea about your bedroom decor? Just jot it or sketch it on a sticky-note and place it here till you have time to pursue the idea!

Are your bedside table drawers filled with swatches and paint chips? Tape them here and you'll always know the right shades or patterns for touch-ups or new accents.

Did you see something exciting in a magazine? Paper clip the photo, article, craft idea, or advertisement right here so you can keep it handy! (Be sure to check the magazine classified section for discount supply houses and their 60-75 percent savings!)

Has someone passed on names of talented and reasonably priced paper hangers or painters? Tape their business cards and brochures here so that you can take bids whenever you need them.

Do you have "before" or "after" photos of your bedroom or shots of you and your family working on home projects? Glue them here so that they will become a part of your home portfolio.

B E D R O O M

Floor

Dimensions _____

_____

Covering _____

_____

_____

Windows

Dimensions _____

_____

_____

Style _____

_____

Fabrics _____

_____

_____

_____

Walls

Dimensions _____

_____

_____

_____

Wallcovering _____

_____

_____

Paint _____

_____

_____

Trim

Style/Type _____

_____

Stain/Paint _____

Built-ins

Dimensions _____

_____

_____

Stain/Paint _____

_____

Furnishings

Name	Brand/Style	Value

Linens

Manufacturer	Pattern

CHILDREN'S

Have an interesting idea about your child's bedroom? Just jot it or sketch it on a sticky-note and place it here till you have time to pursue the idea!

Are your dresser drawers filled with swatches and paint chips? Tape them here and you'll always know the right shades or patterns for touch-ups or new accents.

Did you see something exciting in a magazine? Paper clip the photo, article, craft idea, or advertisement right here so you can keep it handy! (Be sure to check the magazine classified section for discount supply houses and their 60-75 percent savings!)

Has someone passed on names of talented and reasonably priced craftspeople? Tape their business cards and brochures here so that you can take bids as soon as you need them.

Do you have "before" or "after" photos of the bedroom or shots of you and your family working on home projects? Glue them here so that they will become a part of your home portfolio.

B E D R O O M

FLOOR

Dimensions _____

_____

Covering _____

_____

_____

WINDOWS

Dimensions _____

_____

_____

Style _____

_____

Fabrics _____

_____

_____

_____

WALLS

Dimensions _____

_____

_____

_____

Wallcovering _____

_____

_____

Paint _____

_____

_____

TRIM

Style/Type _____

_____

Stain/Paint _____

BUILT-INS

Dimensions _____

_____

_____

Stain/Paint _____

_____

_____

FURNISHINGS

Name	Brand/Style	Value

LINENS

Manufacturer	Pattern

Have an interesting idea about your guest bedroom? Just jot it or sketch it on a sticky-note and place it here till you have time to pursue the idea!

Are your dressing table drawers filled with swatches and paint chips? Tape them here and you'll always know the right shades or patterns for touch-ups or new accents.

Did you see something exciting in a magazine? Paper clip the photo, article, craft idea, or advertisement right here so you can keep it handy! (Be sure to check the magazine classified section for discount supply houses and their 60-75 percent savings!)

Has someone passed on names of talented and reasonably priced craftspeople? Tape their business cards and brochures here so that you can take bids whenever you need them.

Do you have "before" or "after" photos of the bedroom or shots of you and your family working on home projects? Glue them here so that they will become a part of your home portfolio.

B E D R O O M

Floor

Dimensions _____

_____

Covering _____

_____

_____

Windows

Dimensions _____

_____

_____

Style _____

_____

Fabrics _____

_____

_____

Walls

Dimensions _____

_____

_____

_____

Wallcovering _____

_____

_____

Paint _____

_____

_____

Trim

Style/Type _____

_____

Stain/Paint _____

Built-ins

Dimensions _____

_____

_____

Stain/Paint _____

_____

_____

Furnishings

Name	Brand/Style	Value

Linens

Manufacturer	Pattern

Have an interesting idea about your bathroom decor? Just jot it or sketch it on a sticky-note and place it here till you have time to pursue the idea!

Are your linen closet shelves filled with swatches and paint chips? Tape them here and you'll always know the right shades or patterns for touch-ups or new accents.

Did you see something exciting in a magazine? Paper clip the photo, article, craft idea, or advertisement right here so you can keep it handy! (Be sure to check the magazine classified section for discount supply houses and their 60-75 percent savings!)

Has someone passed on names of talented and reasonably priced re-glazers or tile-setters? Tape their business cards and brochures here so that you can take bids as soon as you need them.

Do you have "before" or "after" photos of your bathroom or shots of you and your family working on home projects? Glue them here so that they will become a part of your home portfolio.

BATHROOM

Floor

Dimensions _____

_____

Covering _____

_____

Windows

Dimensions _____

_____

Style _____

_____

Fabrics _____

_____

Walls

Dimensions _____

_____

_____

Wallcovering _____

_____

Paint _____

_____

Cabinetry

Dimensions _____

_____

_____

Stain/Paint _____

_____

_____

Counters

Dimensions _____

_____

Covering _____

_____

Trim

Style/Type _____

_____

Stain/Paint _____

_____

Fixtures

Name	Manufacturer	Value

Built-ins

Dimensions _____

_____

Stain/Paint _____

_____

Linens

Manufacturer	Pattern

Have an interesting idea about your decor in the extra bathroom? Just jot it or sketch it on a sticky-note and place it here till you have time to pursue the idea!

Are your vanity drawers filled with swatches and paint chips? Tape them here and you'll always know the right shades or patterns for touch-ups or new accents.

Did you see something exciting in a magazine? Paper clip the photo, article, craft idea, or advertisement right here so you can keep it handy! (Be sure to check the magazine classified section for discount supply houses and their 60-75 percent savings!)

Has someone passed on names of talented and reasonably priced plumbers or mirror cutters? Tape their business cards and brochures here so that you can take bids whenever you need them.

Do you have "before" or "after" photos of your bathroom or shots of you and your family working on home projects? Glue them here so that they will become a part of your home portfolio.

BATHROOM

Floor

Dimensions _____
_____

Covering _____

Windows

Dimensions _____
_____

Style _____
_____

Fabrics _____
_____

Walls

Dimensions _____
_____
_____

Wallcovering _____
_____

Paint _____
_____

Cabinetry

Dimensions _____
_____
_____

Stain/Paint _____
_____
_____

Counters

Dimensions _____
_____

Covering _____
_____

Trim

Style/Type _____
_____

Stain/Paint _____
_____

Fixtures

Name	Manufacturer	Value

Built-ins

Dimensions _____
_____

Stain/Paint _____
_____

Linens

Manufacturer	Pattern

GLOSSARY

Accent Colors. Contrasting colors used to enliven a room decorating scheme.

Accent Lighting. Decorative spot lighting used for mood, not for utility.

Alkyd Paint. A hard top coat paint, solvent based, used for wood or metal surfaces, interior or exterior.

Analogous Colors. Colors that are next to one another on a color wheel, such as green and blue-green.

Architectural Glass Blocks. Solid glass blocks which can be used individually as decorating pieces or stacked for a window or interior accent wall.

Art Grouping. A collection of matching or coordinating framed prints, photos, or other decorative items displayed on a wall as one item.

Bandbox. Any sturdy paper box, such as a hat box, with a lid.

Band Saw. A fixed table or floor saw used for cutting intricate shapes and curves.

Bolt. A length of woven fabric, usually 2 to 25 yards long, depending on the weight of the fabric. Standard widths are 45 and 60 inches.

Burlap. A strong, heavy, loosely-woven fabric, usually made from jute or hemp fibers.

Cafe Curtains. Informal double or triple tiered curtains which cover only the bottom half of a window and are usually shirred on a rod or hung from decorative rings threaded on a curtain rod.

Canopy. A covering, usually of fabric, suspended on poles or hung above a bed.

Canvas. A closely woven, heavy fabric, usually of cotton, available bleached or unbleached and in a variety of weights. Heavier weights may require a heavy-duty sewing machine to stitch.

Casement Window. Window style that opens in or out from hinges on the side.

Complementary Colors. Colors that are opposite one another on a color wheel, such as purple and yellow.

Cording. Purchased piping, covered with fabric, used to make a neat, decorative edge along the seam of pillows or sofa cushions.

Chair Rail. A linear trim, usually of wood, placed around a room at the approximate height of the back of a chair. A chair rail effect can be produced with a wallpaper border.

Clerestory Window. Small window placed high on a wall, overlooking an adjacent roof. (Pronounced "clear-story").

Craft Paint. General term used to describe any number of different paint products available in craft or hobby stores. Type of paint needed depends on the surface being painted.

Crown Molding. A linear wood trim with a molded edge used around a room at ceiling height to add interest and depth to a room.

Dado. The portion of a wall beneath a chair rail, often decorated to contrast with the portion above. (Pronounced "DAY-doe").

Dowel Rod. A round wooden rod usually of small diameter.

Dry Brushing. A painting process wherein a clean, dry paint brush is dragged through a wet paint surface, producing a lightly grained effect.

Eclectic. A decorating style which combines furnishings and accessories of various types and periods in a harmonious and pleasing manner.

Enamel Paint. A high-gloss, hard-wearing paint, usually used as a decorative and protective top coat.

Essential Oils. Any plant oil which possesses the scent or other characteristic of the plant, such as lemon or rose oil. Usually found in craft and health food stores.

Faille. A soft, ribbed fabric of silk, rayon, or lightweight taffeta particularly good for draperies or table skirts. (Pronounced "fayl").

Faux. Term used to describe a surface that has been treated or designed to give it the appearance of another, as in faux marble. (Pronounced "foe").

Fiberoptic Tubing. Lighting source composed of hair-thin glass fibers twisted into flexible and light-weight cables.

Finial. Architectural detail or ornament. Also describes decorative end-piece on curtain rods or on top of the harp in a table lamp. (Pronounced "FIN-e-uhl").

Focal Point. A visual center of interest in a room, such as an architectural detail, an impressive piece of furniture, or a fireplace.

Formica. A trademarked name for a plastic used as a heat-proof covering for counter tops, furniture, etc.

Gilding. A painting process wherein a thin coat of gold-color glaze is applied and rubbed off a carved wood surface giving an antique finish.

Grasscloth. A wall covering material made from natural grasses woven with cotton and glued to a paper backing. Especially useful for adding texture or covering uneven wall surfaces.

Grit. Term used to describe the relative coarseness of sandpaper. Standard grits run from 400 (super fine) to 60 (coarse).

Incandescent Lighting. Term used to describe any light source employing a traditional light bulb.

Jabot. A pleated length of fabric hung decoratively either under or over the swag or sides of the valance on a window treatment. (Pronounced "Juh-BOW").

Jig Saw. A narrow, hand-held power saw, mounted vertically, used for cutting curves or other difficult lines.

Jute. A strong, coarse plant fiber used for making burlap or rope. Often used as a backing on carpet.

Kiwi Twigs. A new and popular natural accent. Naturally twisted vines from the kiwifruit, found in craft and floral shops.

Lacquer. A protective coating, such as varnish, used to produce a highly polished, lustrous finish on wood or other surfaces.

Lamé. A decorative, ornamental fabric often made of silk, wool, or rayon, with interwoven metallic threads. (Pronounced "luh-MAY").

Laminate. Building material formed of a succession of thin layers pressed and glued together. Often a lesser grade of wood is used for inside layers, with a better grade of wood for top layer.

Latex Paint. A water-based paint generally used for interior walls and ceilings.

Library Table. Large, usually wooden table with one or more drawers. Usually has 2 or 4 pedestal legs.

BATHROOMS AND KITCHENS

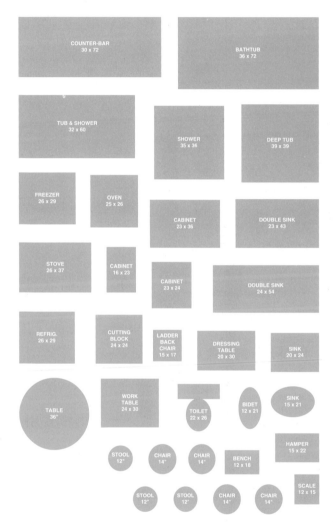

Make a copy of the furniture templates. Cut out the individual pieces which apply to your room and move the pieces around on the graph paper until you determine the appropriate new design for your room.

You'll find that moving these pieces around on paper is a lot easier than moving the real pieces around your room.

Bedrooms

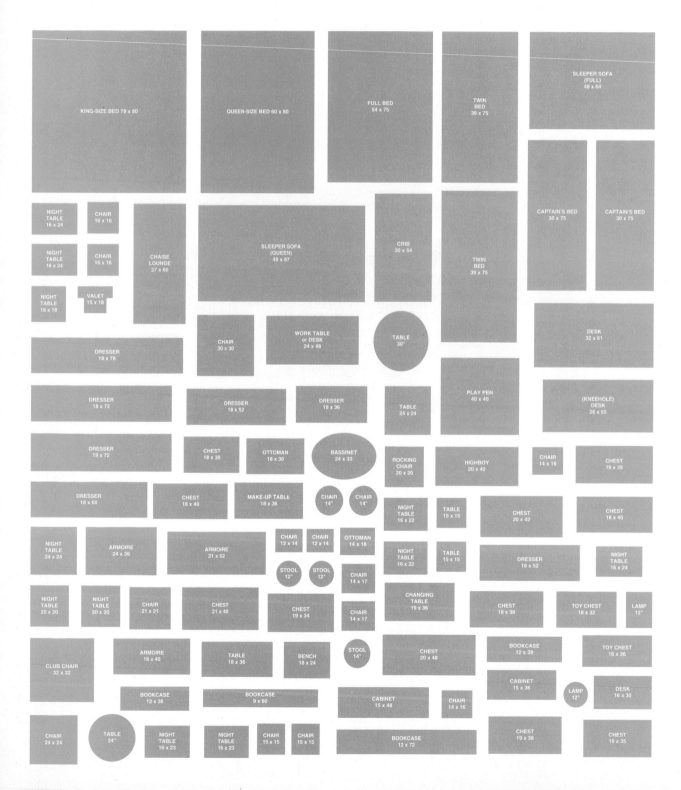

KING-SIZE BED 78 x 80

QUEEN-SIZE BED 60 x 80

FULL BED
54 x 75

TWIN
BED
39 x 75

SLEEPER SOFA
(FULL)
48 x 64

NIGHT
TABLE
16 x 24

CHAIR
16 x 16

NIGHT
TABLE
16 x 24

CHAIR
16 x 16

CHAISE
LOUNGE
27 x 60

SLEEPER SOFA
(QUEEN)
48 x 87

CRIB
30 x 54

CAPTAIN'S BED
30 x 75

CAPTAIN'S BED
30 x 75

TWIN
BED
39 x 75

NIGHT
TABLE
18 x 18

VALET
15 x 18

CHAIR
30 x 30

WORK TABLE
or DESK
24 x 48

TABLE
30"

DESK
32 x 61

DRESSER
18 x 78

DRESSER
18 x 72

DRESSER
18 x 52

DRESSER
18 x 36

TABLE
24 x 24

PLAY PEN
40 x 40

(KNEEHOLE)
DESK
26 x 55

DRESSER
19 x 72

CHEST
18 x 30

OTTOMAN
18 x 30

BASSINET
24 x 33

ROCKING
CHAIR
20 x 20

HIGHBOY
20 x 42

CHAIR
14 x 16

CHEST
19 x 39

DRESSER
18 x 60

CHEST
18 x 40

MAKE-UP TABLE
18 x 36

CHAIR
14"

CHAIR
14"

NIGHT
TABLE
16 x 22

TABLE
15 x 15

CHEST
20 x 42

CHEST
18 x 40

NIGHT
TABLE
24 x 24

ARMOIRE
24 x 36

ARMOIRE
21 x 52

CHAIR
12 x 14

CHAIR
12 x 14

OTTOMAN
14 x 18

NIGHT
TABLE
16 x 22

TABLE
15 x 15

DRESSER
18 x 52

NIGHT
TABLE
16 x 24

STOOL
12"

STOOL
12"

CHAIR
14 x 17

NIGHT
TABLE
20 x 20

NIGHT
TABLE
20 x 20

CHAIR
21 x 21

CHEST
21 x 40

CHEST
19 x 34

CHAIR
14 x 17

CHANGING
TABLE
19 x 36

CHEST
18 x 38

TOY CHEST
18 x 32

LAMP
12"

CLUB CHAIR
32 x 32

ARMOIRE
18 x 40

TABLE
18 x 36

BENCH
18 x 24

STOOL
14"

CHEST
20 x 48

BOOKCASE
12 x 39

TOY CHEST
16 x 36

CABINET
15 x 36

LAMP
12"

DESK
16 x 30

BOOKCASE
12 x 36

BOOKCASE
9 x 60

CABINET
15 x 48

CHAIR
14 x 16

CHAIR
24 x 24

TABLE
24"

NIGHT
TABLE
16 x 23

NIGHT
TABLE
16 x 23

CHAIR
15 x 15

CHAIR
15 x 15

BOOKCASE
12 x 72

CHEST
19 x 38

CHEST
19 x 35

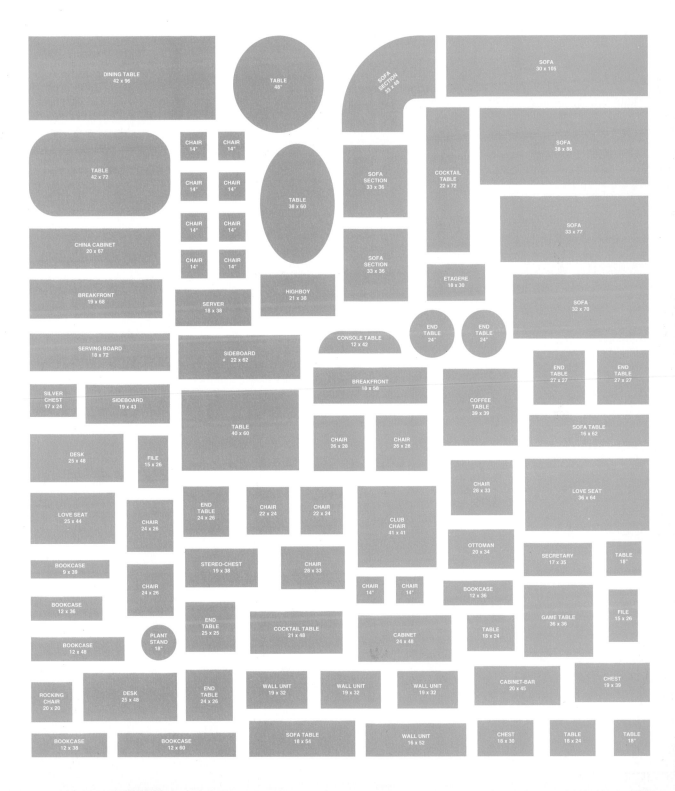

DINING TABLE
42 x 96

TABLE
48"

SOFA
SECTION
33 x 48

SOFA
30 x 105

CHAIR
14"

CHAIR
14"

SOFA
38 x 88

TABLE
42 x 72

CHAIR
14"

CHAIR
14"

SOFA
SECTION
33 x 36

COCKTAIL
TABLE
22 x 72

TABLE
38 x 60

CHAIR
14"

CHAIR
14"

SOFA
33 x 77

CHINA CABINET
20 x 67

CHAIR
14"

CHAIR
14"

SOFA
SECTION
33 x 36

ETAGERE
18 x 30

SOFA
32 x 70

BREAKFRONT
19 x 68

SERVER
18 x 38

HIGHBOY
21 x 38

SERVING BOARD
18 x 72

SIDEBOARD
22 x 62

CONSOLE TABLE
12 x 42

END
TABLE
24"

END
TABLE
24"

BREAKFRONT
18 x 58

END
TABLE
27 x 27

END
TABLE
27 x 27

SILVER
CHEST
17 x 24

SIDEBOARD
19 x 43

COFFEE
TABLE
39 x 39

TABLE
40 x 60

SOFA TABLE
16 x 62

DESK
25 x 48

FILE
15 x 26

CHAIR
26 x 28

CHAIR
26 x 28

CHAIR
28 x 33

LOVE SEAT
36 x 64

LOVE SEAT
25 x 44

CHAIR
24 x 26

END
TABLE
24 x 26

CHAIR
22 x 24

CHAIR
22 x 24

CLUB
CHAIR
41 x 41

OTTOMAN
20 x 34

SECRETARY
17 x 35

TABLE
18"

BOOKCASE
9 x 39

STEREO-CHEST
19 x 38

CHAIR
28 x 33

CHAIR
24 x 26

CHAIR
14"

CHAIR
14"

BOOKCASE
12 x 36

GAME TABLE
36 x 36

FILE
15 x 26

BOOKCASE
12 x 36

END
TABLE
25 x 25

COCKTAIL TABLE
21 x 48

CABINET
24 x 48

TABLE
18 x 24

PLANT
STAND
18"

BOOKCASE
12 x 48

ROCKING
CHAIR
20 x 20

DESK
25 x 48

END
TABLE
24 x 26

WALL UNIT
19 x 32

WALL UNIT
19 x 32

WALL UNIT
19 x 32

CABINET-BAR
20 x 45

CHEST
19 x 39

BOOKCASE
12 x 38

BOOKCASE
12 x 60

SOFA TABLE
18 x 54

WALL UNIT
16 x 52

CHEST
18 x 30

TABLE
18 x 24

TABLE
18"

BATHROOMS AND KITCHENS

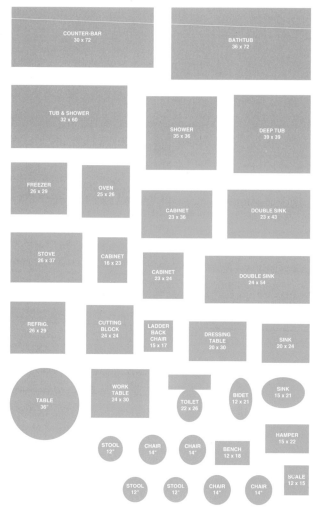

Luminary. An outdoor light source consisting of a small votive candle inside a decorated piece of pottery or metal can or other container such as a brown paper bag filled with sand.

Marbling. A painting process used to simulate the colors and veining of a natural marble surface.

Muslin. An inexpensive cotton fabric of plain weave often used for sheeting.

Occasional Chair. Term used to describe any type of small, extra chair used primarily as an accent piece.

Origami. A Japanese technique of folding paper into decorative or representational shapes, such as birds or animals (Pronounced "OR-e-GAH-me").

Ottoman. A low, upholstered seat, which is armless and backless, often used as a footstool.

Paint Sealer. A product used as a top coat on a painted surface to provide a more time-and weather-resistant finish.

Paladian Window. Dramatic window style featuring a half-circle, non-opening window over a regular double-hung window or sliding glass doors.

Papier-Mâché. A substance made of layers of torn or shredded paper, glued and pressed together, used to form various objects.

Parquet. Different colors or types of wood, inlaid in a geometric pattern, available in squares for flooring.

Pickling. A painting process wherein mineral spirits and white paint are rubbed into a previously painted or stained surface; used to produce an antique or worn-looking finishing on a wood surface.

Pillar Candle. A candle of any height that is the same diameter at the wick end as at the bottom.

Pinking Shears. Scissors with notched blades which allow the edge of a piece of fabric to be finished with a zig-zag cut.

Plantation Blinds. Wide wooden slats strung on cords like traditional Venetian blinds. Can also be Plantation Shutters if fixed in a wooden frame.

Polished Cotton. A cotton or cotton-blend fabric which has been finished to give it a crisp, shiny appearance.

Primer. A first coat applied to a wood surface to seal the pores and provide a smooth undercoat for finishing.

Puddling. Term for the fabric from long window drapes that flows onto the floor and creates a soft "puddled" effect.

Raffia. A palm with long, plume-like leaves which are stripped into fibers used for decorative tying and basket making.

Ragging. A painting process wherein a crumpled rag, paper, or other material is dabbed across a wet paint surface producing a textured, broken-color effect.

Remnants. Shorter lengths of fabric left over after the majority of the fabric on the bolt has been sold.

Roman Shades. Classic, tailored blinds that fold into neat, horizontal pleats when raised.

Rosette. A rose-shaped arrangement of ribbon or gathered fabric used for decorating.

Sisal. A plant fiber (also called sisal hemp) used for making ropes, rugs, or wall coverings.

Stencilling. A decorative painting process wherein different colors of paint are applied through a pattern which has been cut in a thin cardboard or metal plate.

Stippling. A painting process wherein a wet-paint surface is dabbed lightly with a brush, rag, sponge, or crumpled paper adding texture to the surface.

Stripper. Term used to describe chemical function or heat-based products used to remove paint or old wallpaper from a surface.

Sponging. A painting process wherein a natural sponge is used to lightly apply a second color to a neutral painted background, giving the finish a mottled effect.

Swag. A loosely gathered fabric topping for a window treatment which is draped over the curtain rod and allowed to hang down either side of the window.

Tablescape. An individually created, artistic table decoration using 3 or more items arranged as a single unit. May be used on top of or underneath a table or both.

Taper Candle. Tall, traditional shaped candles that taper to a narrow point at the wick end.

Tapestry Needle. A needle used for needlepoint and cross-stitch, of medium length with a long eye and a blunt point which allows it to easily slip between fabric yarns.

Terra Cotta. A hard, kiln-fired clay, reddish-brown colored; used for flowerpots or architectural details. May be used to refer to the color.

Torchier. A freestanding floor lamp which produces an indirect source of light by bouncing the light off the ceiling. (Pronounced "tore-CHEAR").

Tulle. A thin, fine, netted fabric usually made of acetate, nylon, rayon, or silk. (Pronounced "tool").

Topiary. A plant or vine, clipped, twisted, or otherwise formed into an unusual, decorative shape. (Pronounced "TOE-pee-airy").

Utility Knife. A handy, all-purpose knife with a replaceable blade.

Valance. A ruffled or pleated short topping for formal window treatments which hides the drapery track or mini-blind and provides a more finished appearance.

Valance Box. A fixed, wooden box, painted or covered with fabric, or wallpaper; used as a topping for windows.

Votive Candle. Short, round candles usually used in containers arranged in decorative groupings.

Wall Sconce. A lighting fixture with a back plate which attaches directly to a wall. Also called wall light or wall bracket. Provides indirect lighting.

Wardrobe. A piece of furniture that combines drawers with a place for hanging clothes.

Woodgraining. A painting process which produces a surface similar in grain and color to natural wood.

Welt. A trim made of fabric, used to edge a cushion or pillow, giving it a crisp, tailored appearance.

Wood Sealer. Any number of different products which are used to finish a piece of wood and provide a more time-and weather-resistant surface.

Wood Stains. Any number of different products which are used to add color to wood without covering up the natural grain. Depending on the type of wood, stain can be oil-, solvent-, or water-based.

1/4"=1'

PROJECT INDEX

Almond Blossom Ragged Walls, 98
Antiqued and Stencilled Wardrobe, 46
Art from Copied Images, 101

Bandana Curtain, 43
Basket of Antiqued Fruit and Silk Greenery, 58
Bathroom Curtains, 11
Bedside Picture Frame, 63
Bird's Nest in the Brush, 129
Botanical Prints, 98
Bounty from the Sea, 36
Bow Picture Hanger, 96
Broken Tile Floor, 85
Built-in Window Seat, 114
Bundled and Stacked Broom Bloom, 130
Bunny and Lily Arrangement, 138
Bunny Fireplace Screen, 47
Burlap Sack Container, 130
Burlap-Wrapped Vase, 137

Checkboard Pickled Floor with Borders, 88
Children's Places
  Antiqued and Stencilled Wardrobe, 46
  Bandana Curtain, 43
  Bounty from the Sea, 36
  Bunny Fireplace Screen, 47
  Cork-Covered Folding Screen, 113
  Covered Wagon Bed Canopy, 40
  Cowboy Boot Table Lamp, 44
  Cowboy Frames, 44
  Fishy Lampshade, 36
  Giant Origami Figures, 32
  High Plains Mural, 40
  How to Improve a Child's Closet, 33
  How to Wire a Lamp, 45
  Lasso Trash Can, 39
  Leather-Look Pencil Holder, 43
  Painted Bluebird Accent, 112
  Painted Crib and Rocker, 47
  Painted Stepladder, 33
  Painted Sticks, 32
  Papier-Mâché Bowls, 32
  Rag-Painted Child's Desk, 43
  Sheer Crib Drape, 47
  Spattered Chair and Step Stool, 35
  Spatter-Painted Medicine Cabinet, 39
  Starfish Switchplate, 39

  Toy Storage Tubs, 33
Colorful Spheres, 68
Conch Shell Centerpieces, 134
Containers
  Burlap Sack Container, 130
  Burlap-Wrapped Vase, 137
  Conch Shell Centerpieces, 134
  Grapevine Vase, 129
  Marbleized Wooden Bowl, 61
  Papier-Mâché Bowls, 32
  Plaster Floral Container, 62
  Stacked Glass Blocks Floral Display, 122
  Stone-Look Flowerpots, 64
  Terra-Cotta Pot with Raffia and Natural Accents, 132
Coordinated Art Grouping, 103
Cork-Covered Folding Screen, 113
Covered Wagon Bed Canopy, 40
Cowboy Boot Table Lamp, 44
Cowboy Frames, 44
Crackle-Finish Drape Rosettes, 9
Crested Throw Pillows, 71

Desert Garden in a Rock, 137
Draped Bed, 123
Dried Flower Topiary, 130
Dried Fruit Slices, 17
Dropped Wallpaper Border, 112

Easy Two-Fabric Jabot, 14
Extra Easy Walls
  Almond Blossom Ragged Walls, 98
  Art from Copied Images, 101
  Botanical Prints, 98
  Bounty from the Sea, 36
  Coordinated Art Grouping, 103
  Covered Wagon Bed Canopy, 40
  Dropped Wallpaper Border, 112
  Heavenly Painted Ceiling, 112
  High Plains Mural, 40
  How to Prepare Walls, 95
  How to Rag with Paint, 101
  Lilac and Grape Ragged Walls, 107
  Magnolia Art Drape, 97
  Marbleized Lower Walls, 123
  Mirror in Gilded Frame, 103
  Navy Drybrush Wall Treatment, 107
  Painted Bluebird Accent, 112
  Potato Print Stamps, 93
  Ragged Bathroom Wall, 100
  Romantic Bed Drape, 100

  Scrunched Fabric Headboard, 103
  Starfish Switchplate, 39
  Textured and Stencilled Sunroom Walls, 94

Fabric-Covered Ottoman, 64
Fast and Fancy Windows
  Bandana Curtain, 43
  Bathroom Curtains, 11
  Built-in Window Seat, 114
  Crackle-Finish Drape Rosettes, 9
  Easy Two-Fabric Jabot, 14
  Gathered Sheer Curtains, 12
  Herb-Accented Kitchen Sheers, 16
  How to Hang Mini-Blinds, 20
  No-Sew Curtain, 26
  Playroom Window Valance, 23
  Polished Cotton Floral and Striped Curtain, 12
  Puddled Curtain with Rosettes, 24
  Raised Sheer Curtains, 122
  Recovered Valances, 20
  Sheer Roman Blind, 18
  Striped Window Valance, 21
  Swagged Curtains, 10
  Window Drape from Nature, 136
  Window Seat Curtain, 16
Faux Marble Pedestal, 97
Fishy Lampshade, 36
Floral
  Basket of Antiqued Fruit and Silk Greenery, 58
  Bird's Nest in the Brush, 129
  Bundled and Stacked Broom Bloom, 130
  Bunny and Lily Arrangement, 138
  Desert Garden in a Rock, 137
  Dried Flower Topiary, 130
  Ivy Topiary, 75
  Kiwi Twig Arrangemnt, 128
  Moss-Covered Tabletop Topiary, 139
  Painted Dried Weeds, 131
  Pussy Willow, Scotch Broom, and Herbs, 136
  Rag Doll Garden Party, 134
  Rose and Bridal Wreath Spirea Arrangement, 138
  Silk Lilac Topiary, 69
  Stacked Glass Blocks Floral Display, 122
  Window Drape from Nature, 136
Floral Bandbox, 69

Gathered Sheer Curtains, 12
Giant Origami Figures, 32
Gilded Napkin Rings, 62
Gold Leaf Bookstand, 75
Gold Leaf Shell, 75
Gold-Twined Fruit-and-Herb Balls, 98
Grapevine Birdcage, 133
Grapevine Vase, 129

Heavenly Painted Ceiling, 112
Herb-Accented Kitchen Sheers, 16
High Plains Mural, 40
How to Create Faux Marble with Paint, 58
How to Hang Mini-Blinds, 20
How to Improve a Child's Closet, 33
How to Install a Dimmer Switch, 113
How to Prepare Vines, 129
How to Prepare Walls, 95
How to Rag with Paint, 101
How to Refinish a Wood Floor, 86
How to Sponge Paint, 54
How to Stencil, 84
How to Use Natural Accents, 139
How to Wire a Lamp, 45

Illusions of Space
  Built-in Window Seat, 114
  Cork-Covered Folding Screen, 113
  Draped Bed, 123
  Dropped Wallpaper Border, 112
  Heavenly Painted Ceiling, 112
  Marbleized Lower Walls, 123
  Painted Bluebird Accent, 112
  Raised Sheer Curtain, 122
  Stacked Glass Blocks Floral Display, 122
  Type Tray Screen, 114
Ivy Topiary, 75

Kiwi Twig Arrangement, 128

Lasso Trash Can, 39
Leather-Look Pencil Holder, 43
Library Coffee Table, 69
Lilac and Grape Ragged Walls, 107
Linen Bathroom Accent, 75

Magnolia Art Drape, 97
Marbleized Coffee Table, 64
Marbleized Columns, 61
Marbleized Lower Walls, 123
Marbleized Mantel, 59
Marbleized Wooden Bowl, 61
Minute Makeover
  The Bathroom, 77
  The Dining Room, 56
  The Guest Room, 109
  The Kitchen, 143
  The Master Bedroom, 125
  The Nursery, 48
  The Porch, 28
Mirror in Gilded Frame, 103
Moss-Covered Tabletop
  Topiary, 139

Natural Accents
  Bird's Nest in the
    Brush, 129
  Bundled and Stacked Broom
    Bloom, 130
  Bunny and Lily
    Arrangement, 138
  Conch Shell
    Centerpieces, 134
  Desert Garden in a
    Rock, 137
  Dried Flower Topiary, 130
  Dried Fruit Slices, 17
  Gold Leaf Shell, 75
  Gold-Twined Fruit-and-
    Herb Balls, 98
  Grapevine Birdcage, 133
  Grapevine Vase, 129
  How to Prepare Vines, 129
  How to Use Natural
    Accents, 139
  Kiwi Twig Arrangement, 128
  Magnolia Art Drape, 97
  Moss-Covered Tabletop
    Topiary, 139
  Painted Dried Weeds, 131
  Painted Grasses and
    Flowers, 137
  Painted Sticks, 32
  Potpourri-Filled Moss
    Basket, 141
  Pussy Willow, Scotch Broom,
    and Herbs, 136
  Rag Doll Garden Party, 134
  Rose and Bridal Wreath Spirea
    Arrangement, 138
  Seashell Mirror, 134
  Willow Branches in
    Basket, 128

Window Drape from
  Nature, 136
Navy Drybrush Wall
  Treatment, 107
No-Fuss Floors
  Broken Tile Floor, 85
  Checkboard Pickled Floors
    with Borders, 88
  How to Refinish a Wood
    Floor, 86
  How to Stencil, 84
  Painted Canvas
    Floorcloth, 80
  Painted Floor, 80
  Spatter-Painting a Floor, 87
  Stencilled Nursery Floor, 84
  Stencilled Sisal Rug, 83
  Woodgraining, 85
No-Sew Curtain, 26

Painted Bluebird Accent, 112
Painted Canvas Floorcloth, 80
Painted Canvas Table
  Runner, 55
Painted Crib and Rocker, 47
Painted Dried Weeds, 131
Painted Floor, 80
Painted Grasses and
  Flowers, 137
Painted Stepladder, 33
Painted Sticks, 32
Papier-Mâché Bowls, 32
Pillows
  Alternating Squares
    Pillow, 118
  Back Cushions, 118
  Crested Throw Pillows, 71
  Envelope Pillow, 67
  Fan-Shaped Pillow, 66
  Lace Strip Pillow, 66
  Plaid Couch Cushions, 72
  Stripe Tucked Pillow, 119
  Tucked Throw Pillows, 118
  Window Seat Cushions, 118
  Windowpane Pillow, 119
Pillows from Old Linens, 66
Plaid Couch Cushions, 72
Plaster Floral Container, 62
Playroom Window
  Valance, 23
Polished Cotton Floral and
  Striped Curtain, 12
Potato Print Stamps, 93
Potpourri-Filled Moss
  Basket, 141
Puddled Curtain with
  Rosettes, 24

Pussy Willow, Scoth Broom,
  and Herbs, 136

Rag Doll Garden Party, 134
Rag-Painted Child's Desk, 43
Ragged Bathroom Wall, 100
Raised Sheer Curtain, 122
Recovered Armchair, 66
Recovered Valances, 20
Recycled Accents
  Art from Copied Images, 101
  Basket of Antiqued Fruit and
    Silk Greenery, 58
  Bedside Picture Frame, 63
  Botanical Prints, 98
  Burlap Sack Container, 130
  Burlap-Wrapped Vase, 137
  Colorful Spheres, 68
  Cork-Covered Folding
    Screen, 113
  Cowboy Boot Table Lamp, 44
  Cowboy Frames, 44
  Crested Throw Pillows, 71
  Fabric-Covered Ottoman, 64
  Faux Marble Pedestal, 97
  Fishy Lampshade, 36
  Floral Bandbox, 69
  Gilded Napkin Rings, 62
  Gold Leaf Bookstand, 75
  Gold Leaf Shell, 75
  Grapevine Vase, 129
  Lasso Trash Can, 39
  Leather-Look Pencil
    Holder, 43
  Library Coffee Table, 69
  Linen Bathroom Accent, 75
  Marbleized Coffee Table, 64
  Marbleized Wooden Bowl, 61
  Mirror in Gilded Frame, 103
  Painted Crib and Rocker, 47
  Painted Stepladder, 33
  Pillows from Old Linens, 66
  Plaid Couch Cushions, 72
  Potpourri-Filled Moss
    Basket, 141
  Rag-Painted Child's Desk, 43
  Recovered Armchair, 66
  Reupholstered Chair Seats, 62
  Roomy Tub Tray, 74
  Seashell Mirror, 134
  Sheer Crib Drape, 47
  Spattered Chair and Step
    Stool, 35
  Spindle Candlesticks, 60
  Sponge-Painted Outdoor
    Furniture, 52
  Stencilled Lampshade, 120

Stone-Look Flowerpots, 64
Tabletop Luminaries, 55
Torchère Luminaries, 52
Type Tray Screen, 114
Watering Can Luminary, 81
Reupholstered Chair Seats, 62
Romantic Bed Drape, 100
Roomy Tub Tray, 74
Rose and Bridal Wreath Spirea
  Arrangement, 138
Round Tablecloth, 71

Scrunched Fabric
  Headboard, 103
Seashell Mirror, 134
Sheer Crib Drape, 47
Sheer Roman Blind, 18
Silk Lilac Topiary, 69
Spatter-Painted Medicine
  Cabinet, 39
Spatter-Painting a Floor, 87
Spattered Chair and Step
  Stool, 35
Spindle Candlesticks, 60
Sponge-Painted Outdoor
  Furniture, 52
Sponged Plaster Frame
  Ensemble, 96
Stacked Glass Blocks Floral
  Display, 122
Starfish Switchplate, 39
Stencilled and Painted Tub, 74
Stencilled Lampshade, 120
Stencilled Nursery Floor, 84
Stencilled Sisal Rug, 83
Stone-Look Flowerpots, 64
Striped Window Valance, 21
Swagged Curtains, 10

Tabletop Luminiaries, 55
Terra-Cotta Pot with Raffia and
  Natural Accents, 132
Textured and Stencilled
  Sunroom Walls, 94
Torchère Luminaries, 52
Toy Storage Tubs, 33
Type Tray Screen, 114

Watering Can Luminary, 81
Willow Branches in Basket, 128
Window Drape from
  Nature, 136
Window Seat Curtain, 16
Window Seat Cushions, 118
Woodgraining, 85

HERITAGE HOUSE, INC., a division of The Southwestern Company, offers a varied selection of porcelain collectibles. For details on ordering, please write: Heritage House, Inc., P.O. Box 305147, Nashville, TN 37230

PHOTOGRAPH INDEX

Cover
Photographer: Bill LaFevor
Photo Stylist: Fran Zinder
Designer: Fran Zinder
  Scrunched Fabric
    Headboard, 103–105
  Lilac and Grape Ragged
    Walls, 107
  Snack tray and setting by
    Pier 1 Imports, Inc.
Page 3
Photographer: Bill LaFevor
Photo Stylist: Miriam Myers
Designer: Chris Gates
  Willow Branches in Basket, 128
  Rag Doll Garden Party, 134
Designer: Julie Rolin
  Grapevine Birdcage, 133
Designer: Miriam Myers
  Painted Canvas
    Floorcloth, 80-81
  Burlap Sack Container, 130
Designer: Charlotte Hagood
  Watering Can Luminary, 81–83
Designer: Kathleen English
  Terra-Cotta Pot with Raffia and
    Floral Accents, 132
  Additional furnishings by
    Pier 1 Imports, Inc.
Page 7
Photographer: Bill LaFevor
Photo Stylist: Fran Zinder
Designer: Fran Zinder
  Window Seat Curtain, 16
  Built-In Window Seat, 114–116
Designer: Charlotte Hagood
  Window Seat Back
    Cushions, 118
  Tucked Throw Pillow, 118
  Stripe Tucked Pillow, 119
  Alternating Squares
    Pillow, 118-119
  Windowpane Pillow, 119
Designer: Jack Wood
  Stencilled Lampshade, 120
  Tea Setting and accessories by
    Pier 1 Imports, Inc.
Pages 8–9
Photographer: Bill LaFevor
Photo Stylist: Fran Zinder
Designer: Laura Hill
  Marbleized Columns, 61
Designer: Fran Zinder
  Swagged Curtains, 10
  Reupholstered Chair
    Seats, 62–63
Designer: Carol Tipton
  Crackle-Finish Drape
    Rosettes, 9
  Spindle Candlesticks, 60

Plaster Floral Container, 62
Designer: Chris Gates
  Rose and Bridal Wreath Spirea
    Arrangement, 138
Designer: Kathleen English
  Gilded Napkin Rings, 63
Page 11
Photographer: Bill LaFevor
Photo Stylist: Miriam Myers
Designer: Miriam Myers
  Bathroom Curtains, 11-12
  Roomy Tub Tray, 74
  Ragged Bathroom Wall, 100
  Stencilled and Painted Tub, 74
Designer: Jack and Maribel Wood
  Gold Leaf Shell, 75
  Gold Leaf Bookstand, 75
  Bundled florals by
    Pier 1 Imports, Inc.
Page 13
Photographer: Bill LaFevor
Photo Stylist: Miriam Myers
Designer: Miriam Myers
  Gathered Sheer Curtains, 12
  Painted Canvas Table
    Runner, 55
  Marbleized Lower Walls, 123
Designer: Chris Gates
  Basket of Antiqued Fruit and
    Silk Greenery, 58–59
  Place settings by
    Pier 1 Imports, Inc.
Page 14
Photographer: Bill LaFevor
Photo Stylist: Miriam Myers
Designer: Miriam Myers
  Polished Cotton Floral and
    Striped Curtain, 12
  Recovered Armchair, 66
  Dropped Wallpaper
    Border, 112–113
Designer: Charlotte Hagood
  Potpourri-Filled Moss
    Basket, 141
Designer: Heidi King
  Bedside Picture Frame, 63–64
Designer: Chris Gates
  Stone-Look Flowerpots, 64
  Moss-Covered Tabletop
    Topiaries, 139
Pillows by Pier 1 Imports, Inc.
Page 15
Photographer: Bill LaFevor
Photo Stylist: Miriam Myers
Designer: Miriam Myers
  Easy Two-Fabric Jabot, 14–15
Designer: Teresa Moll
  Window Drape From
    Nature, 136
Designer: Mary Steverson

Silk Lilac Topiary, 69
Designer: Heidi King
  Floral Bandbox, 69
Page 17
Photographer: Bill LaFevor
Photo Stylist: Miriam Myers
Designer: Chris Gates and
Miriam Myers
  Herb-Accented Kitchen
    Sheers, 16–17
Designer: Miriam Myers
  Dried Fruit Slices, 17–18
  Selected accent pieces by
    Pier 1 Imports, Inc.
Page 19
Photographer: Bill LaFevor
Photo Stylist: Miriam Myers
Designer: Miriam Myers
  Sheer Roman Blind, 18
  Stacked Glass Blocks Floral
    Display, 122
Designer: Steve Sanford
  Checkerboard Pickled Floor
    with Borders, 88–89
Page 21
Photographer: Bill LaFevor
Photo Stylist: Fran Zinder
Designer: Fran Zinder
  Navy Drybrush Wall
    Treatment, 107
  Recovered Valances, 20-21
Page 22
Photographer: Bill LaFevor
Photo Stylist: Fran Zinder
Designer: Fran Zinder
  Striped Window Valance, 21
  Potato Print Stamps, 93–94
Designer: Chris Gates
  Kiwi Twig Arrangement, 128
  Place settings by
    Pier 1 Imports, Inc.
Page 23
Photographer: Bill LaFevor
Photo Stylist: Fran Zinder
Designer: Fran Zinder
  Playroom Window Valance, 23
Page 24-25
Photographer: Bill LaFevor
Photo Stylist: Fran Zinder
Designer: Laura Hill
  Almond Blossom Ragged
    Walls, 98
Designer: Fran Zinder
  Puddled Curtain with
    Rosettes, 24
  Romantic Bed Drape, 100
Designer: Charlotte Hagood
  Pillows from Old
    Linens, 66–67
  Botanical Prints, 98

Designer: Chris Gates
  Gold-Twined Fruit-and-
    Herb Balls, 98
  Bed linens and carpet by
    Pier 1 Imports, Inc.
Page 26
Photographer: Bill LaFevor
Photo Stylist: Miriam Myers
Designer: Miriam Myers
  No-Sew Curtains, 26
Pages 28-29
Photographer: Bill LaFevor
Photo Stylist: Miriam Myers
Designer: Chris Gates
  Willow Branches in
    Basket, 128
  Rag Doll Garden Party, 134
Designer: Julie Rolin
  Grapevine Birdcage, 133
Designer: Miriam Myers
  Painted Canvas
    Floorcloth, 80-81
  Burlap Sack Container, 130
Designer: Charlotte Hagood
  Watering Can
    Luminary, 81-83
Designer: Kathleen English
  Terra-Cotta Pot with Raffia
    and Floral Accents, 132
  Additional furnishings by
    Pier 1 Imports, Inc.
Page 31
Photographer: Bill LaFevor
Photo Stylist: Fran Zinder
Designer: Tory Powell
  Giant Origami Figures, 32
  For more information on
  origami, send an SASE to
  Friends of the Origami Center
  of America
  Attn: Phyllis Meth
  4005 166th Street
  Flushing, NY 11358
Designer: Fran Zinder
  Papier Mâché Bowls, 32
  Painted Sticks, 32
  Toy Storage Tubs, 33
  Playroom Window
    Valance, 23
  Painted Stepladder, 33–35
  Photo frames by
    Pier 1 Imports, Inc.
Page 34
Photographer: Bill LaFevor
Photo Stylist: Fran Zinder
  Painted Stepladder, 33–35
  Painted Sticks, 32
  Toy Storage Tubs, 33
  Photo frames by
    Pier 1 Imports, Inc.

Page 36-37
Company: Imperial Wallcoverings
  Spattered Chair and Step
    Stool, 35
  Fishy Lampshade, 36 and 39
  Starfish Switchplate, 39
  Spatter-Painted Medicine
    Cabinet, 39
  Bounty from the Sea, 36
Page 38
Company: Imperial Wallcoverings
Page 40-41
Photographer: Bill LaFevor
Photo Stylist: Fran Zinder
Designer: Fran Zinder
  Lasso Trash Can, 39
  High Plains Mural, 40-43
  Cork-Covered Folding
    Screen, 113-114
Designer:
  Sallie and John Starbuck, ASID
  Covered Wagon Bed
    Canopy, 40
  Standing saguaro metal art by
  Jack Wood, pillows by
  Bobbie Weisman, rocking horse
  by Russ Jacobsohn.
Page 42
Photographer: Bill LaFevor
Photo Stylist: Fran Zinder
  Desert Garden in a Rock, 137
Designer: Fran Zinder
  Lasso Trash Can, 39
  Cowboy Frames, 44-45
  Leather-Look Pencil Holder, 43
  Cowboy Boot Table Lamp, 44
  Bandana Curtain, 43
  Rag-Painted Child's
    Desk, 43–44
  Horseshoe cowboy art by Jack
  Wood, desk chair cushion by
  Bobbie Weisman.
Page 46
Photographer: Bill LaFevor
Photo Stylist: Miriam Myers
Designer: Miriam Myers
  Stencilled Nursery Floor, 84
  Antiqued and Stencilled
    Wardrobe, 46
  Painted Crib and Rocker, 47
  Bunny Fireplace Screen, 47
Page 48-49
Photographer: Bill LaFevor
Photo Stylist: Miriam Myers
Designer: Miriam Myers
  Stencilled Nursery Floor, 84
  Antiqued and Stencilled
    Wardrobe, 46
  Painted Crib and Rocker, 47
  Heavenly Painted Ceiling, 112
  Painted Bluebird Accent, 112
  Bunny Fireplace Screen, 47
  Sheer Crib Drape, 47
  No-Sew Curtain, 26
Designer: Chris Gates
  Bunny and Lily
    Arrangement, 138-139
  Birdcage and pillows by
  Pier 1 Imports, Inc.

Page 51
Photographer: Bill LaFevor
Photo Stylist: Fran Zinder
Designer: Fran Zinder
  Sponge-Painted Outdoor
    Furniture, 52
  Torchere Luminaries, 52-55
  Tabletop Luminaries, 55
  Hand-painted divider screen by
  Maggie Sanford.
  Assorted accent pieces by
  Pier 1 Imports, Inc.
Page 52-53
Photographer: Bill LaFevor
Photo Stylist: Miriam Myers
Designer: Fran Zinder
  Sponge-Painted Outdoor
    Furniture, 52
  Torchere Luminaries, 52-55
  Tabletop Luminaries, 55
Designer: Miriam Myers
  Painted Canvas
    Floorcloth, 80-81
  Assorted accent pieces by
  Pier 1 Imports, Inc.
Page 55
Photographer: Bill LaFevor
Photo Stylist: Miriam Myers
Designer: Miriam Myers
  Painted Table Runner, 55
Designer: Chris Gates
  Basket of Antiqued Fruit and
    Silk Greenery, 58-59
Pages 56-57
Photographer: Bill LaFevor
Photo Stylist: Miriam Myers
Designer: Miriam Myers
  Gathered Sheer Curtains, 12
  Painted Canvas Table Runner, 55
  Marbleized Lower Walls, 123
Designer: Chris Gates
  Basket of Antiqued Fruit and
    Silk Greenery, 58-59
  Place settings by
  Pier 1 Imports, Inc.
Page 59
Photographer: Bill LaFevor
Photo Stylist: Miriam Myers
Designer: Chris Gates
  Ivy Topiary, 75
Designer: Mary Steverson
  Silk Lilac Topiary, 69
Designer: Miriam Myers
  Marbleized Mantel, 59
Page 60
Photographer: Bill LaFevor
Photo Stylist: Fran Zinder
Designer: Carol Tipton
  Spindle Candlesticks, 60
  Marbleized Wooden Bowl, 61
Page 61
Photographer: Bill LaFevor
Photo Stylist: Fran Zinder
Designer: Laura Hill
  Marbleized Columns, 61
Page 63
Photographer: Bill LaFevor
Photo Stylist: Fran Zinder
Designer: Carol Tipton

Plaster Floral Container, 62
Designer: Chris Gates
  Rose and Bridal Wreath Spirea
    Arrangement, 138
Designer: Kathleen English
  Gilded Napkin Rings, 62
Designer: Fran Zinder
  Reupholstered Chair Seats, 62
Page 64
Photographer: Bill LaFevor
Photo Stylist: Miriam Myers
Designer: Charlotte Hagood
  Potpourri-Filled Moss
    Basket, 141
Designer: Heidi King
  Bedside Picture Frame, 63-64
Designer: Chris Gates
  Stone-Look Flowerpots, 64
  Moss-Covered Tabletop
    Topiaries, 139-140
Designer: Miriam Myers
  Marbleized Coffee Table, 64
Page 65
Photographer: Bill LaFevor
Photo Stylist: Miriam Myers
Designer: Miriam Myers
  Fabric-Covered Ottoman, 64–65
  Recovered Armchair, 66
Page 67
Photographer: Bill LaFevor
Photo Stylist: Fran Zinder
Designer: Charlotte Hagood
  Pillows from Old Linens, 66-67
Page 68
Photographer: Trevor Barrett
Designer: Michael Zurhorst
Page 70
Photographer: Bill LaFevor
Photo Stylist: Fran Zinder
Designer: Heidi King
  Colorful Spheres, 68–69
Designer: Fran Zinder
  Library Coffee Table, 69
Designer: Charlotte Hagood
  Crested Throw Pillows, 71
  Assorted accent pieces by
  Pier 1 Imports, Inc.
Page 72-73
Photographer: Bill LaFevor
Photo Stylist: Fran Zinder
Designer: Chris Gates
  Painted Dried Weeds, 131
  Bundled and Stacked Broom
    Bloom, 130
Designer: Heidi King
  Colorful Spheres, 68-69
Designer: Fran Zinder
  Recovered Valances, 20-21
  Library Coffee Table, 69
  Navy Drybrush Wall
    Treatment, 107
  Round Tablecloth, 71
Designer: Charlotte Hagood
  Crested Throw Pillows, 71
  Plaid Couch Cushions, 72
  Selected furnishings and accent
  pieces by Pier 1 Imports, Inc.
Page 74
Photographer: Bill LaFevor

Photo Stylist: Miriam Myers
Designers: Jack and Maribel
Wood
  Golf Leaf Bookstand, 75
  Gold Leaf Shell, 75
Designer: Miriam Myers
  Roomy Tub Tray, 74
  Stencilled and Painted
    Tub, 74–75
  Linen Bathroom Accent, 75
Pages 76
Photographer: Bill LaFevor
Photo Stylist: Miriam Myers
Designer: Miriam Myers
  Ragged Bathroom Wall, 100
  Coordinated Art Grouping, 103
  Art from Copied Images, 101
  Bathroom Curtains, 11-12
  Roomy Tub Tray, 74
  Mirror in Gilded Frame, 103
  Stencilled and Painted Tub, 74
Designer: Chris Gates
  Pussywillow, Scotch Broom,
    and Herbs, 136-137
Designers: Jack and Maribel
Wood
  Gold Leaf Shell, 75
  Gold Leaf Bookstand, 75
  Bundled florals by
  Pier 1 Imports, Inc.
Page 79
Photographer: Bill LaFevor
Photo Stylist: Miriam Myers
Designer: Steve Sanford
  Painted Floor, 80
  Woodgraining, 85–87
Page 81
Photographer: Bill Myers
Photo Stylist: Miriam Myers
Designer: Charlotte Hagood
  Watering Can Luminary, 81–83
Designer: Miriam Myers
  Burlap Sack Container, 130
  Painted Canvas
    Floorcloth, 80-81
Page 82
Photographer: Bill LaFevor
Photo Stylist: Miriam Myers
Designer: Charlotte Hagood
  Stencilled Sisal Rug, 83
  Accent pillows by
  Pier 1 Imports, Inc.
Page 84
Photographer: Bill LaFevor
Photo Stylist: Miriam Myers
Designer: Miriam Myers
  Stencilled Nursery Floor, 84
Pages 88-89
Photographer: Bill LaFevor
Photo Stylist: Miriam Myers
Designer: Steve Sanford
  Checkerboard Pickled Floor
    with Borders, 88-89
Designer: Miriam Myers
  Stacked Glass Blocks Floral
    Display, 122
Page 91
Designer: Dennis Jenkins and
Sunny McLean

Textured and Stencilled
Sunroom Walls, 94
Page 92-93
Photographer: Bill LaFevor
Photo Stylist: Fran Zinder
Designer: Chris Gates
Kiwi Twig Arrangement, 128
Designer: Fran Zinder
Potato Print Stamps, 93-94
Striped Window Valance, 21
Place settings and assorted
furnishings by
Pier 1 Imports, Inc.
Page 96
Photographer: Bill LaFevor
Photo Stylist: Miriam Myers
Designer: Charlotte Hagood
Bow Picture Hanger, 96
Framed print by
Pier 1 Imports, Inc.
Page 97
Photographer: Bill LaFevor
Photo Stylist: Miriam Myers
Designer: Chris Gates
Magnolia Art Drape, 97
Designer: Miriam Myers
Faux Marble Pedestal, 97
Framed print by
Pier 1 Imports, Inc.
Page 99
Photographer: Bill LaFevor
Photo Stylist: Fran Zinder
Designer: Laura Hill
Almond Blossom Ragged
Walls, 98
Designer: Fran Zinder
Romantic Bed Drape, 100
Designer: Chris Gates
Gold-Twined Fruit-and-Herb
Balls, 98
Designer: Charlotte Hagood
Botanical Prints, 98
Page 100
Photographer: Bill LaFevor
Photo Stylist: Fran Zinder
Designer: Fran Zinder
Romantic Bed Drape, 100
Designer: Charlotte Hagood
Pillows from Old Linens, 66-67
Bed linens by
Pier 1 Imports, Inc.
Page 102
Photographer: Bill LaFevor
Photo Stylist: Miriam Myers
Designer: Miriam Myers
Art from Copied Images, 101
Coordinated Art Grouping, 103
Ragged Bathroom Wall, 100
Designer: Chris Gates
Pussy Willow, Scotch Broom,
and Herbs, 136–137
Page 104-105
Photographer: Bill LaFevor
Photo Stylist: Fran Zinder
Designer: Fran Zinder
Scrunched Fabric
Headboard, 103-105
Lilac and Grape Ragged
Walls, 107

Snack tray and setting by
Pier 1 Imports, Inc.
Page 106
Photographer: Bill LaFevor
Photo Stylist: Fran Zinder
Designer: Chris Gates
Painted Grasses and
Flowers, 137
Designer: Heidi King
Burlap-Wrapped Vase, 137
Page 107
Photographer: Bill LaFevor
Photo Stylist: Fran Zinder
Designer: Fran Zinder
Navy Drybrush Wall
Treatment, 107
Pages 108-109
Photographer: Bill LaFevor
Photo Stylist: Miriam Myers
Designer: Miriam Myers
Polished Cotton Floral and
Striped Curtain, 12
Recovered Armchair, 66
Fabric-Covered Ottoman, 64–65
Dropped Wallpaper
Border, 112-113
Designer: Charlotte Hagood
Potpourri-Filled Moss
Basket, 141
Designer: Heidi King
Bedside Picture Frame, 63–64
Designer: Chris Gates
Stone-Look Flowerpots, 64
Moss-Covered Topiaries, 139
Pillows and fireside topiary by
Pier 1 Imports, Inc.
Page 111
Photographer: Bill LaFevor
Photo Stylist: Fran Zinder
Designer: Fran Zinder
Lasso Trash Can, 39
High Plains Mural, 40-43
Cork-Covered Folding
Screen, 113-114
Designer:
Sallie and John Starbuck, ASID
Covered Wagon Bed Canopy,
Pillows by Bobbie Weisman.
Page 112
Photographer: Bill LaFevor
Photo Stylist: Miriam Myers
Designer: Miriam Myers
Heavenly Painted Ceiling, 112
Painted Bluebird Accent, 112
Page 115
Photographer: Bill LaFevor
Photo Stylist: Fran Zinder
Designer: Fran Zinder
Type Tray Screen, 114
Designer: Chris Gates
Birds' Nest in the Brush, 129
Page 116
Photographer: Bill LaFevor
Photo Stylist: Fran Zinder
Designer: Fran Zinder
Window Seat Curtain, 16
Built-In Window
Seat, 114–116
Designer: Charlotte Hagood

Window Seat Back
Cushions, 118
Tucked Throw Pillow, 118
Stripe Tucked Pillows , 119
Alternating Squares
Pillow, 118–119
Windowpane Pillow, 119
Designer: Jack Wood
Stencilled Lampshade, 120
Tea Setting and accessories by
Pier 1 Imports, Inc.
Page 121
Company: Imperial Wallcoverings
Page 122
Photographer: Trevor Barrett
Designer: Michael Zurhorst
Page 124-125
Photographer: Bill LaFevor
Photo Stylist: Miriam Myers
Designer: Miriam Myers
Draped Bed, 123
Raised Sheer Curtain, 122
Designer: Charlotte Hagood
Bow Picture Hanger, 96
Designer: Heidi King
Grapevine Vase, 129
Page 126
Photographer: Bill LaFevor
Photo Stylist: Fran Zinder
Designer: Fran Zinder
Type Tray Screen, 114
Designer: Chris Gates
Birds' Nest in the Brush, 129
Page 128
Photographer: Bill LaFevor
Photo Stylist: Miriam Myers
Designer: Miriam Myers
Marbleized Lower Walls, 123
Designer: Chris Gates
Willow Branches in
Basket, 128
Page 131
Photographer: Bill LaFevor
Photo Stylist: Fran Zinder
Designer: Chris Gates
Painted Dried Weeds, 131
Bundled and Stacked Broom
Bloom, 130
Designer: Fran Zinder
Recovered Valances, 20-21
Navy Drybrush Wall
Treatment, 107
Round Tablecloth, 71
Library Coffee Table, 69
Designer: Heidi King
Colorful Spheres, 68-69
Selected furnishings and accent
pieces by Pier 1 Imports, Inc.
Page 132-133
Photographer: Bill LaFevor
Photo Stylist: Miriam Myers
Designer: Chris Gates
Willow Branches in Basket, 128
Rag Doll Garden Party, 134
Designer: Julie Rolin
Grapevine Birdcage, 133
Designer: Miriam Myers
Painted Canvas
Floorcloth, 80–81

Designer: Kathleen English
Terra-Cotta Pot with Raffia
and Floral Accents, 132
Additional furnishings by
Pier 1 Imports, Inc.
Page 135
Photographer: Trevor Barrett
Designer: Michael Zurhorst
Page 136
Photographer: Bill LaFevor
Photo Stylist: Miriam Myers
Designer: Miriam Myers
Ragged Bathroom Wall, 100
Coordinated Art Grouping, 103
Art from Copied Images, 101
Bathroom Curtains, 11–12
Roomy Tub Tray, 74
Mirror in Gilded Frame, 103
Stencilled and Painted Tub, 74
Designer: Chris Gates
Pussywillow, Scotch Broom,
and Fresh Herbs, 136-137
Designers:
Jack and Maribel Wood
Gold Leaf Shell, 75
Gold Leaf Bookstand, 75
Bundled florals by
Pier 1 Imports, Inc.
Page 138
Photographer: Bill LaFevor
Photo Stylist: Miriam Myers
Designer: Chris Gates
Bunny and Lily
Arrangement, 138
Designer: Miriam Myers
Stencilled Nursery Floor, 84
Page 140-141
Photographer: Bill LaFevor
Photo Stylist: Miriam Myers
Designer: Miriam Myers
Polished Cotton Floral and
Striped Curtain, 12
Recovered Armchair, 66
Dropped Wallpaper
Border, 112–113
Designer: Charlotte Hagood
Potpourri-Filled Moss
Basket, 141
Designer: Heidi King
Bedside Picture Frame, 63-64
Designer: Chris Gates
Moss-Covered Tabletop
Topiaries, 139
Stone-Look Flowerpots, 64
Pillows by Pier 1 Imports, Inc.
Page 142-143
Photographer: Bill LaFevor
Photo Stylist: Miriam Myers
Designer: Chris Gates and
Miriam Myers
Herb-Accented Kitchen
Sheers, 16–17
Designer: Miriam Myers
Dried Fruit Slices, 17–18
Selected accent pieces by
Pier 1 Imports, Inc.
Selection of featured merchandise
at Pier 1 Imports, Inc. may vary
depending on store location.